THE CURSE
OF THE
GIANT TORTOISE

TRAGEDIES, MYSTERIES
AND CRIMES
IN THE

GALAPAGOS
ISLANDS

OCTAVIO LATORRE
Quito - Ecuador
1990

AUTHOR: Dr. Octavio Latorre T.
Translators: Dr. Patricia Netherly, Mrs. Judy Dickinson
de Salomón and Mrs. Kyle Cummins.
Unifying version: Dr. Patricia Netherly.
Final Revision of the Manuscript: Dr. Patricia Netherly,
Mrs. Judy Dickinson de Salomón and Mrs. Mary
Goodman de Laínez.
Photographs: Carlos Mora.
DERECHOS RESERVADOS.

To my dear ones:

**Rosario, Orlando, José Luis
and
Carlos**

Octavio Latorre has been studying for quite a
number of years the History of Galapagos
Islands and that of the discovery and
colonization of the Amazon.
Some of his works been published and
others are in print.
-"La Cartografïa del Amazonas. S. XVIII". 1988.
-El Pequeño Imperio de Manuel J. Cobos en
Galapagos", in print.
-Tomás de Berlanga, descubridor de Galapagos.
-La Cartografía Histórica de Galapagos.

THE CURSE OF THE GIANT TORTOISE is the history
of the tragic colonization process over
the centuries in the Galapagos Islands. The main
purpose of the Author in writing this book
is the protection of the ecology of the
Archipielago from a wanton destruction on the
name of "Civilization".

THE CURSE OF THE GIANT TORTOISE in the press:

"We may affirm that this book is one of the most interesting
written in Spanish about human history of the ENCHANTED
ISLANDS. It is a valuable piece of research and at the same time
a fascinating encounter with the old mysterious world of Galapagos.

EL TELEGRAFO, Guayaquil, July 8, 1990.

CONTENTS

CONTENTS

FOREWORD

THE CURSE OF THE GIANT TORTOISE
THE REASON FOR THIS TITLE

The enchanted islands of the Galapagos hold great secrets, not only for science but also for history. Many events that have made these islands famous could easily serve as inspiration for horror movies and novels. People's imagination, always so rich, could not help but elaborate these frequent bizarre events and search for explanations.

Traveling through the islands many years ago now, I took part in one of those evening get-togethers which were very common before the advent of television. At those after-dinner gather ings, the latest news was passed on, family histories were re—told and finally, ghost stories, enlivened by frequent jokes and commentaries, were traded.

It was on one of these evenings that I first heard the legend of the giant tortoise and its curse, a result, no doubt, of natural observation enhanced by lively imagination.

It is said that if you look into the eyes of these creatures, you will see a gaze that is both mysterious and piercing. Tortoises can remain staring for long periods of time as if wishing to examine life and its purpose. The eyes, which presumedly have stood witness for at least a century, also carry years of experience which enables them to perceive the motives and ambitions of those visiting the islands: weather they come to destroy this peaceful refuge or simply to admire it.

This slow, deep stare of the tortoise marks the approval of the visit or the announcement of the newcomer's death; it is a safe welcome or a curse which will be carried out without fail in the most varied of circumstances.

The tortoise's curse then is not so much an explanation but rather a legendary evocation of the tragic events which ocurred in this marvelous paradise called the Galapagos.

Few places in the world can claim so many tragedies with such unfortunate consequences in so small an area in so short time. It is ironic that such a peaceful kingdom as the Archipelago has been the macabre scene of hate, violence and death, that people were not able to find peace in this paradise until they discover its secret:

> *These islands should not form part of urban mass production or commerce which leaves in its wake, in the name of progress, mountains of garbage, stench and smog.*
> *The enchanted Islands of Galapagos should only be visited, admire and remembered.*

All attempts to exploit the resources of the islands have ended in failure or tragedy, as seen in the efforts of Villamil, Valdizan and Cobos to colonize and even in the most recent case, of the "adventurers" of 1960.

These failures fortunately have saved the beauty and integrity of the islands for science and for those of us who appreciate nature as if directly from the hands of God. Because despite all the damage caused by human settlement, the disturbance produced by introduced animals, and the slaughter of thousands of tortoises and sea lions in the past centuries, one can still appreciate and study a world as it must have been thousands of years ago; a real luxury in a world turned upside –down by the hand of man.

Lack of water has also been providential for the preservation of the ecosystems on the islands and for the defence of the nation's territorial rights as well. The shortage of water stopped the buccaneers and whalers who would surely have taken possession of the islands had they found an abundant supply of water for crops and human consumption. Instead, the pirates and whalers considered the islands only as a temporary refuge; Captain Colnet came to this conclusion in 1793 after he studied the commercial and industrial possibilities of the islands. The same conclusion was reached by Captain Fitzroy after visiting the Archipelago in 1835.

But let us imagine what would have become of the islands had there been an abundance of water. They all would probably have been turned into bare rocks, burned white by the sun with nothing of interest for either the scientist or the tourist. This is what happened when Manuel J. Cobos who in less than 25 years eliminated all tortoises on San Cristobal Island and began to do the same on other islands. What would have happened had there been more human settlements?

The lack of water or "The Curse of the Tortoise" has saved the beauty and integrity of these islands and will continue to preserve this wonderful corner of the world for science and culture.

The gaze of the tortoise, mysterious and deep, seems to hold transfixed the history of centuries of hate, passion, and violence. If these animals could speak they would tell us, with ironic smiles, not only how hundreds of thousands of their brothers and sisters died, but how men who came to the islands searching for riches and power killed each other. They would also tell us, ironically, how the descendants of those that killed off the tortoises are now the most fervent defenders of this evolutionary paradise, as if unconsciously to make up for wanton destruction in the past. And they would hope that future generations of Ecuadorians, the descendants of those that sacrificed so many tortoises to light the street lights of the mainland, will continue to defend this evolutionary paradise.

THE TORTOISE'S CURSE LEAVES US A MESSAGE THAT WE CANNOT FORGET:

ALL ATTEMPTS AT BLIND EXPLOITATION, WITH NO REGARD FOR THE ENVIRONMENT OF THE ISLANDS, WILL END IN FAILURE OR DEATH.

The narratives which we present are only a selection of the many tragic tales from the Islands, all are true and are based on historical research. Citation to sources and documents had been omitted to retain the flow of the narrative, nevertheless, a list of further readings has been placed at the end of the principle chapters for those readers who wish to read more about those subjects.

Admiration for the Enchanted Islands inspired the collection of these tragic accounts; may they contribute to the conservation of the Galapagos beauty.

ACKNOWLEDGMENTS

The Author is happy to record his sincere thanks to friends and acquaintances for invaluable help and much kindness: to Mr. and Mrs. Thomas Cummins, Mrs. Judy Dickinson de Salomón, Mrs. Mary Goodman de Laínez and Dr. Patricia Netherly for their translation and final correction of the manuscript; to Mr. Jacinto Gordillo from the Isabela island for first hand information about the penal colony and Almiral (Ret) Carlos Monteverde for the additional interesting facts about the recent tragedies in the islands; to the Charles Darwin Foundation and more particularly to Juan Black its former secretary for the invitation to study in Santa Cruz Station's Library, and finally to own family who encouraged me to continue in my research and readings.

GALAPAGOS ISLANDS

I.PINTA (Abingdon)

Punta Mejía

MARCHENA (Bindloe)

GENOVESA (Tower)

Volcán Wolf

Volcán Darwin

Equinoccial

Volcán Alcedo

Volcán Ecuador

FERNANDINA (Narborough)

SANTIAGO-SAN SALVADOR (James)

RABIDA (Jervis)

PINZON (Duncan)

Daphne

N.Seymour

BALTRA(S.Seymour)

I.Plaza

Academy Bay

SANTA CRUZ.Chavez. (Indefatigable)

SANTA FE (Barrington)

Volcán Sierra Negra

S.Tomás

Puerto Villamil

Cerro

ISABELA (Albemarle)

SANTA MARIA -FLOREANA (Charles)

Post Office

Black Beach

ESPAÑOLA (Hood)

SAN CRISTOBAL (Chatham)

Progreso

Baquerizo Moreno

Wreck Bay

CHAPTER I

VOYAGES OF NO RETURN AND THE DISCOVERY OF THE GALAPAGOS

The first tragic tales of the Galapagos begin in prehistoric time with the voyages of no return by indians from the Ecuadorian coast. The inhabitants of the coast were great seamen and, on their balsa rafts, they could leave the rivers behind and head for the open sea. Archaeologists have found much evidence of the indians' ability: bone from fish from the open sea are found in food remains; there are clear indications of interregional maritime trade, which probably extended to Central America in the north and to Chile in the south.

Balsa rafts can carry heavy cargos. They can navigate in open seas because of their vertical rudders or dagger boards (guares), which, in addition to increasing the rafts' stability, allow them to take advantage of the currents and advance by tacking. A raft thus equipped was capable of cruising the ocean and carrying the news of 'Perú to Panamá, where the Spanish must have heard it from the mouths of the voyagers themselves. The audacity of these mariners must have ended tragically more than once when they were carried by the Humboldt Current towards the Galapagos or out to sea.

The discovery on the islands of prehistoric artifacts is testimony to these visits and probable tragedies, since the sailors never returned. The ability of the balsa rafts to tack is limited and it is difficult to imagine a return of over 1,000 kilometers, sailing against the current (1).

We will never know the terrible end of these voyages, but we

(1) Some sailing vessels which made the crossing from the Galapagos to Guayaquil during the last century and the beginning of this one frequently took several weeks to cross the Humboldt Current when the wind was against them. Tomás de Berlanga himself took 24 days to return to the mainland in 1535.

can imagine the frightful death from thirst and hunger on the desolate islands.

The only presumed round—trip voyage to the Islands would be the one described by Miguel Sarmiento de Gamboa in 1572. According to him, Topa Inga Yupanqui (Tupac Inka Yupanki) organized a maritime expedition with part of his army and returned at the end of a year with much gold and silver, a horse's jawbone, and people with dark skins, among other things.

THE BALSA RAFT OF GUAYAQUIL, seen by Alexander von Humboldt.

The navigating capability of the balsa raft made voyages to the Galapagos and beyond possible.

Modern scholarship has removed all historic truth from this incredible journey, supposedly made by a mountain people who always feared the water. To become sailors overnight happens more readily in the realm of fantasy than in the real world. Moreover, the objects brought from the distant islands reveal the suspiciousness of the account: abundant gold and silver are not to be found on lava islands; still less likely are dark—skinned people, unless the chronicler had confused them with sun—bronzed survivors of shipwrecks.

Sarmiento de Gamboa belongs to the group of chroniclers called "Toledan", that is, at the service of policies of Viceroy Francisco de Toledo, one of the goals of which was the justification of the rights of Spain to the Inca empire and, above all, the legitimacy of the will imposed on the last Inca heir in which he bequeathed the Inca empire to King Phillip the Second. Sarmiento was to write a history (?) which justified the possession by the Inca of the lands of their empire.

Friend of the occult and persecuted for this by the Inquisition in Lima, Sarmiento included in his narrative a "necromancer" who had visited the islands previously in a lightning flight to ensure the practicality of the Inca's voyage. The relation of the Toledan chronicler definitely belongs to the realm of fantasy.

* * *

The first expedition of discovery was made by Tomás de Berlanga in March, 1535 and was also involuntary. We call it an expedition of discovery because he reached the islands and returned to describe them and leave his record. Tomás de Berlanga was the fourth Bishop of Panamá and was sent to Perú on an important and difficult mission which can be summarized in three parts: to set the boundaries between the areas to be governed by Pizarro and Almagro; to review the accounts of the Conqueror of Perú and the royal officials of the treasure captured in the new lands; and, finally, to report on the new regions incorporated into the Spanish Crown.

TOMAS DE BERLANGA, Bishop of Panamá.

He discovered the Galapagos Archipelago during a mission to Perú to review the accounts
of Pizarro and to stablish the boundaries of his territory. Berlanga belonged to the group
of Dominican missionaries which, in 1508, protested the injusticies of the Conquistado-
res and even dared to question the right of Spain to invade America.

Tomás de Berlanga was chosen for this complex mission by the King because of his ability and prudence, despite the fact that in 1508 he was one of the first group of missionaries which had dared to protest against the injustices of the conquerers and encomenderos and even questioned the right of Spain to invade the American continent. As Superior of the monastery of Santo Domingo, he had received Fray Bartolomé de las Casas into the community in 1521. Berlanga was, then, an independent person in thought and action and by the same token the man called upon to face the conquerers of Perú.

America owes him much and Ecuador even more. He was one of the fathers of the Panamá Canal, he introduced many useful plants to the continent, particularly the banana. Moreover, Ecuador owes him, in addition to the discovery of the Archipelago, for the suggestion to the King of Spain in January 1536 that a "**Gobernación**" of Quito be created, which constitutes the basis for Ecuadorian nationhood.

The ship carrying Berlanga sailed from Panamá on the 23rd of February 1535. During the first days of the voyage the wind was favorable. However, they were becalmed off the Chocó. The sails hung limply from the masts and there was not the least breeze for three weeks. The ship was carried to the southwest by the Panamá Current, which appears at this time of year. When hope for surviving was all but lost, an island was sighted and optimism was renewed. In time they reached the beach where they had to bury a man who had died of thirst and several horses. Another man died on the island. These were the first sacrifices to the Enchanted Isles.

Water was sought with feverish anxiety, but in vain. The only consolation was to wet the lips on the bitter hearts of cactus. On the horizon, could see a larger, wooded island which led them to believe from its size that it would have rivers and springs. They were delayed by ocean currents and only on the third day could they disembark. It was Saturday and hard as they tried, they could find water nowhere. The water in the ponds was brackish, forcing them back to the cactus, which tasted of lye.

On Sunday March 15th, everyone came on land and, after hearing mass, they began to explore the island in groups of two or three. It was now a question of life or death for those Spaniards who had come to seek treasure. The situation was such that they would have given all of Atahualpa's ramsom for a glass of water. At last they found some pools, left by the last winter rains. They were saved! Several containers were filled with water for the crossing to Perú, which was not far by their calculations, and the ship prepared to sail to the mainland. They saw two other islands, one of them very large (Isabela) and the other smaller, but these were not visited. The impression given by the islands was not very encouraging: they were covered with rocks and lava; there was scarcely soil for meager cultivation. The only attraction was the antidiluvian animals like the "galapago", the "iguana" and the tame birds which were not frightened by the presence of men.

The problems of the discoverers of the Galapagos were far from over. The Humboldt Current checked their progress toward the mainland and carried the ship off course. Within a few days the distraught pilot sought Berlanga for help, because he did not know in what direction they were headed. Since Berlanga knew how to use an astrolabe, he took readings and realized they were heading for the central Pacific. On the course they were sailing, they would surely have reached Australia one day. The ship's course was changed, but thirst made new inroads. The coast of Manabí was sighted, but as progress was slow, it took several days to reach shore and in the meantime one more man died. The others sustained themselves with the last measures of water mixed with wine.

On the 9th of April, 1535 they finally entered the Bay of Caraquez which impressed the voyagers with its beauty and the safety of its harbor. The crossing from the islands had taken 24 days. The sailors rested while Tomás de Berlanga travelled to Porto Viejo where he wrote his famous letter to the King relating the discovery of the Archipelago on the 26th of April 1535.

This letter and the first impressions of the visitors set the limit for the new navigators who would sail these waters after them. Galapagos was not a place to shelter or colonize. On the contrary, these islands were soon to become famous for horror and tragedy.

The following decades were full of references to expeditions which ended tragically in the Galapagos or which cruised through them without finding a drop of water.

In 1546, during the civil war among the conquerers, there ocurred the defeat and flight of Captain Diego de Rivadeneira towards the north. He had been part of the army of Captain Centeno, who sought to defend the rights of the King, but was defeated by Pizarro's men. Fearful of falling into the hands of the blood—thirsty Francisco de Carbajal, Rivadeneira and a few others embarked in a small vessel and sailed northward with scanty provisions and without seamen. The Captain ordered the pilot to sail away from the coast to avoid meeting enemy ships. After sailing 25 days, they sighted land and, believing it was Tumbez or Puná Island, Rivadeneira threw the unfortunate pilot overboard. They barely managed to rescue him after they realized that it was a different island of "wonderful beauty, which appeared to be always covered in mist". "It had many coves and large forests were seen even near the shore and they said there were some who saw . . . smoke and others who did not"(1) They were probably off Isabela Island, the largest and most volcanic in the Archipelago.

Some landed in search of water, but after travelling inland several miles the parties hurriedly returned to the beach, fearful of being left on land. Tragic mistrust bred of the civil wars! Several days later in the midst of a complete calm, an enormous sea turtle was spied floating on the surface and it was decided to capture it, since food was short. A youth volunteered to be lowered in a small boat. While all were watching the maneuver, a strong wind suddenly arose, pushing the vessel to the northeast, forcing them to abandon the poor lad in the immensity of the sea. Possibly the

(1) Jiménez de la Espada. 1892.

lack of seamanship or the mutual distrust brought about the sacrifice of the unhappy youth. Another early victim of the gods of the Galapagos. When Captain Rivadeneira arrived in Guatemala, he sought to claim the rights of discoverer of the islands. However, little importance was given to his claim because, among other reasons, there were rumors of the existence of the islands and the small benefit that could be expected from them.

When Francisco de Quiroz was preparing his expedition for Oceania in 1606, there was talk of a "vessel which was a launch or two—masted **zabra** which had arrived shortly before from the island of the Galapagos, after picking up men who had been lost there. . ."(1).When did this shipwreck happen? was it the one mentioned by Licenciado León Pinelo in 1653 in his life of Saint Toribio? Here is his account:

> Fray Martín de Barragán, lay brother of the same order (Santo Domingo), the terror of hell, the dread of sinners, solid in virtue, a great penitent, was doorkeeper in my time. He was one of those who **spent three years on the island of the Galapagos** which caused his conversion . . .

The imagination fills in the brief account of these marooned men on the empty island; reduced to the most extreme conditions and in such a situation they turned to God as their only hope.

One does not know if it was the same shipwreck. In any case, the first victims of the Galapagos must have been very well—known in Lima and Callao, which were the goal of the expeditions of merchants, conquerers and adventurers.

The "Islands of the Galapagos" remained in the minds of all as a terrible place and this tradition happily saved the islands from devastating exploitation and made possible the discovery of their importance four centuries later.

(1)   Jiménez de la Espada, Marcos: 1892.

ADDITIONAL READINGS

Holm, Olaf:
    La Navegación Precolombina.. Análisis de una leyenda" Boletín Histórico. Quito,
    Ns. 17 - 1982. pp. 125-136.

Jiménez de la Espada,.. Marco
    "Las Islas Galápagos y otras más al Poniente", Madrid, 1892.

Vargas. J.M. etc. al.
    Tomás de Berlanga: Descubridor de Galápagos (En prensa).

G. MERCATOR'S MAP. 1569

This is the first map on which the Galapagos Islands appear. ("Y. de los Galopegos")
in two separate groups. It was copied by various 16th century cartographers.

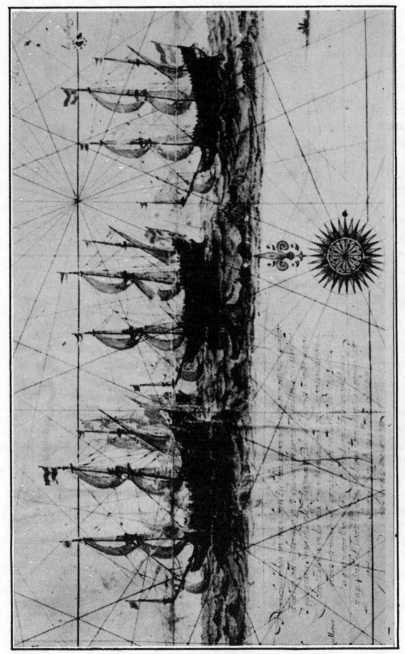

DUTCH SQUADRON SAILING IN THE EASTERN PACIFIC AND GALAPAGOS ISLANDS.

A map by Hessel Guerrits taken from a contemporary Spanish map. It is probably the first to present a close appoximation of the archipelago.

CHAPTER II

PIRATE HIDEAWAY AND GRAVEYARD

The Galapagos were left in peace after the first visits and ship-wrecks of Spanish sailors, perhaps because their memory did not arouse enthusiasm or because better knowledge of sea lanes avoided becalming and involuntary visits.

This did not mean the Galapagos had been altogether forgotten; the Spanish visited them repeatedly and even named some of the islands. These were the "old Spanish names"; among them were La Aguada, Mascarín, La Salud, Tabaco, Dos Hermanos, San Marcos, San Clemente and Santa Isabel. In fact, the route through the Galapagos was being used more often for commerce with Acapulco. Ships could take advantage of the northward—flowing Humboldt Current and then sail north by the shorter route to the west of the islands.

The English pirates used the islands as a safe hideaway after their expeditions to the "Southern Sea" (the Pacific) and as a secure refuge for their attacks on Spanish commerce.

The weakness of Spain and, above all the Spanish navy, made the pirates' task an easy one. They came in large numbers around Cape Horn and even crossed the Isthmus of Panamá to surprise merchant vessels and convoys of galleons carrying the wealth of the Pacific colonies of Spain.

The terrible memory of Drake's catastrophic forays lived on, but dimmed with time. Then came the Dutch pirates Pierre L'Hermite and others. However, the most difficult period for the Spanish colonies came at the end of the 17th century with the return of the English pirates. In 1680 the expeditions led by John Cook, Richard Hawkins, John Watling and Bartholomew Sharp entered the "Southern Sea". Three members of this expedition have left us accounts of the Galapagos Islands: Leonel Wafer, William Dampier and Basil Ringrose. The expediton's visit to the Islands was brief, since they sought water and, not finding any, believed the islands were of little value.

A new expedition returned bringing some of the same men, together with others, who became known this time: Dampier, Wafer, Ambrose Cowley, Edward Davis, and others. After taking on provisions in Chesapeake Bay, they sailed south to the Gulf of Guinea. There, they captured a 36 gun Danish ship which was in better condition than their own. They decided to change ships, renaming the Danish vessel the **Bachelor's** Delight and burning and sinking their old ship to leave no trace. They continued their voyage toward the South Atlantic. On the 14th of February, a terrible irony on the new name of the ship, they were attacked by a fierce storm which lasted several days and almost carried them to Antartica.   Their ship was able to round Cape Horn and enter the Pacific Ocean at the end of March.

A few days later, they encountered another pirate, Captain Eaton, who commanded the Nicholas, and joined forces. Together, the enlarged expedition sailed to Juan Fernandez Island and, after picking up a Mosquito Indian who had been left there three years earlier by Captain Watling, they sailed for the Lobos del Mar Islands off the northern coast of Perú. They repaired their ships and lay in wait for prospective victims. The wait was not pleasant; 140 men were ill, among them Captain Cook.

A week later the pirates fell upon three Spanish merchant ships but their booty held more than one surprise. One of the vessels was carrying a giant statue of the Virgin and a mule, a gift from the Viceroy for the Governor of Panamá. Another carried several tons of quince paste in her hold. Altogether, the booty was nothing to make the pirates happy. Their frustration increased when they learned from their prisoners that they had come within a hairsbreadth of seizing a vessel with 800,000 gold pieces of eight, which had been hurriedly unloaded in Huanchaco at the rumor of the pirates presence.

The advantage of surprise had been lost and the pirates sailed for the Galapagos where they unloaded the 600 jars of quince paste and hid several hundred sacks of flour.(1)

William Dampier and Ambrose Cowley have both left us detailed descriptions of their visits to the Islands. Cowley also made a map which is a good approximation despite his lack of time and knowledge of Cartography. The majority of the English names of the Islands were given by Cowley and remain in use today as the internationally best-known alternate designations.

This expediton found the safe harbors and anchorages which were later used by practically everyone. However, it is not certain that they located sources of water. In any event, the giant tortoise provided excellent food for them on land and later during several months of voyage. These corsairs began the slaughter of the tortoise which lasted until well into the 19th century.

The Archipelago was also to prove to be the final resting place or halbringer of death for countless despoilers. One of the first was Captain Cook himself, followed by several of his companions. Edward Davis, the second in comand, was made Captain of the expedition.

They sailed for Cocos Island and then cruised the coast of Central America and México without finding any important prize. The expedition stationed itself off the Gulf of Panamá to await their luck. There, they met up with another group of pirates which had crossed the Isthmus and siezed several Spanish ships. Among these pirates were captain Swan and the Frenchmen, Crogniet, Rose, Le Picard, and Desmarais; de Lusan arrived a short while later as well. All together, they were a fleet of 10 ships and almost 1000 men. Such a large force alerted the Spanish, who prepared to defend themselves.

(1) Several years ago the jars were found by Ecuadorian explorers and archaeologists, who at first were at a loss to explain the presence of so many ceramic containers. (Presley Norton, personal communication).

DUTCH SHIP OF THE 17th CENTURY

Shortly afterwards, the only engagment took place between the Perú fleet of 14 vessels which had arrived carrying treasure. Since there had been warning, the precious cargo was unloaded and the ships sailed forth to battle. Neither side wanted to engage in a fight to the death since, on the one hand the Spaniards were not carrying treasure and on the other, the they wanted to preserve their vessels to carry the bullion to its destination. After two days of skirmishes and maneuvers, the two fleets separated and the pirate alliance ended in failure. The majority sailed for the Far East and the few who remained haunted the sea lanes to Perú under Edward Davis and the recently—arrived Captain Knight. Together, they returned to the Galapagos to recover the 500 sacks of flour and to provision themselves with water and tortoises. They found that several sacks of flour had been eaten by birds. On this visit the pirates did not leave unscathed; an epidemic carried off several to Eternity.

Edward Davis returned to the islands for the third time in - - 1687, after the sack of Guayaquil in which they had obtained much booty for the ransom of several notables of the city. A complete account was left by L. Wafer, who was present. After repairing the ships and provisioning them with water and turtle meat, the pirates headed south.

They reached the West Indies in 1688 at the time when the British government forbade all its subjects to engage in piracy against the Spanish colonies. Spain and Great Britain had signed a peace treaty and Spanish ports were opened to commerce in English goods. The buccaneers were left unemployed for some time.

Eighteenth Century Pirates

The Engish corsairs returned to America once more during the War of the Spanish Succession (1707—1713). Guayaquil suffered the attack of Woodes Rodgers while the city was recovering from a terrible epidemic. William Dampier participated in this expedition for the third and last time, but as a pilot of one of the pirate ships rather than as a captain.

We will trace the principal stages of this expedition since the Galapagos Islands were one of its centers of activity. Two vessels, the *Duke* and the *Dutchess,* arrived financed by merchants of the port of Bristol. Captain Rodgers commanded the Duke and Captain Courtney the Dutchess. They rounded Cape Horn in 1708 and entered the Pacific. They sailed for the Juan Fernandez Island to repair the ships which had been damaged in the seas off the Horn.

The expedition arrived at Puerto Deseado at sunset where, to everyone's surprise, a light was shining. They believed it might be a French ship which rumored to be in the area. Even greater was the astonishment when at dawn no ship could be seen on the horizon , but on the beach there waited a "man dressed in goatskins who looked wilder than the skins in which he was clothed".

He was a Scotsman who, because of a falling out with Captain Stradling, had been abandoned there four years earlier. He was recognized by Dampier, who said his name was Alexander Selkirk and that he had been considered the best seaman on the earlier expeditions.

Once on board, Selkirk told his fascinated listeners the story of his solitary life during four years and four months on the island. He had been left with a musket, a little powder, shot, and tobacco, as well as with a knife, a hachet, a Bible, and other useful things, such as mathematical instruments and books. The first eight months passed in fear and sadness. when he found himself in such a desolate place. He constantly watched the sea, except when eating and sleeping, as hunger and exhaustion overcame him. He kept a fire going at all times, which gave off heat, light, and even a pleasant fragrance. Little by little, he began to explore the island to throw off his ill humor and sadness. He taught himself to run after the wild goats with incredible speed, which he later demonstrated for his hearers. Once he almost lost his life through this ability to run down the wild goats since he caught up with one at the edge of a cliff which he had not seen; man and goat fell into the chasm. When he recovered consciousness, Selkirk found himself very bruised and sprained on top of the dead goat. He stayed

SPANISH BRIGANTINE OF THE 18th CENTURY

where he was for 24 hours without the strength to move. His hut was a mile away, but he reached it only after hours of painful crawling. He did not leave it for ten days.

To relieve his loneliness he amused himself by cutting his name into the bark of trees and noting down the days of his exile. At first he was much bothered by the cats and rats which had multiplied on the island. The rats, in particular, bit his feet and destroyed his clothing while he slept. The solution was to tame the cats. They slept next to him and kept the area free of rats. He tamed some kids and for amusement danced and sang with them and the cats. Thanks to his strength and Providence, Selkirk, at the age of 30, had managed to conquer solitude and live more tranquilly. When his clothes wore out, he made a sack and a cape of goatskin, sewn with strips of hide. He had no needle, but his knife and his fingernail did the job. When his knife was worn away, he made others from the pieces of iron he found on the beach.

When Selkirk came on board, he could hardly be understood, since he had forgotten how to talk and could scarcely communicate. When he was offered some rum, the drink of every pirate, he could not swallow it since he had drunk nothing but water for four years. It took him some time to regain a taste for rum.

The expedition remained in the Juan Fernandez Island to cure the sick. During this time, Selkirk demonstrated how to catch the goats and thus improve the diet of the invalids.

Once they had recovered, the pirates headed for Guayaquil. On the way they captured several ships and then attacked the city. They demanded 30,000 pesos to free their hostages. They filled the ships with food, wine, and jewels. They headed for the Galapagos with a small group of hostages, for the city had not been able to meet the ransom demanded. They arrived on the 16th of May 1707. The first concern was to find water. Food was easy to get, given the enormous number of giant tortoises.

Since he knew his ability, at Dampier's suggestion, Selkirk was giving command of one of the ships captured in the Gulf of Guayaquil; it was a good choice.

The Galapagos proved to be the fleet's graveyard. They had hardly arrived before a plague broke out in almost all the ships. It soon became clear that the infected were those who had disembarked in Guayaquil.

Woodes Rogers' account of the Galapagos is very clear and is given below, although it is difficult to identify the places he visited.

"May 19th. Yesterday in the afternoon the Boat return'd with a melancholy Account, that no Water was to be found. The Prizes we expected would have lain to Windward for us by the Rock about 2 Leagues off Shore; but Mr. Hatley in a Bark, and the *Havre de Grace,* turn'd to Windward after our Consort the Dutchess; so that only the Galleon and the Bark that Mr. Selkirk was in staid for us . . . At 5 in the Morning we sent our boat ashore again to make a further search in this Island for Water. About 10 in the Morning James Daniel our Joiner died. We had a good Observation, Lat. 00° 32'S.

"May 20. Yesterday in the Evening our Boat return'd but found no Water, tho they went for 3 or 4 miles up into the Country. They tell me the Island is nothing but loose Rocks, like Cynders, very rotten and heavy, and the Earth so parch'd, that it will not bear a Man, but break into Holes under his Feet, which makes me suppose there has been a Vulcano here; tho there is much shrubby Wood, and some Greens on it, yet there's not the least Sign of water, nor is it possible, that any can be contain'd on such a Surface. At 12 last Night we lost sight of our Galleon, so that we have only one Bark with us now.

"May 21 Yesterday in the Afternoon came down the *Dutchess* and the French Prize. The *Dutchess's* Bark had caugth several Turtle and Fish, and gave us a Part, which was very serviceable to the sick Men, our fresh Provisions that we got on the main Land being all spent. They were surpriz'd as much as we at the Galleon, and Hatley's Bark being out of sight, thinking before they had been with us. We kept Lights at our Top—mast's Head, and fir'd Guns all Night, that they might either see or hear how to join us, but to no Purpose.

"Capt. Courtney being not yet quite recover'd, I went on board the *Dutchess*, and agreed with him and his officers, to stay here with the *Havre de Grace* and Bark, whilst I went in Quest of the missing Prizes. At 6 in the morning we parted, and stood on a Wind to the Eastward, judging they lost us that way. Here are very strange Currents amongst these Islands, and commonly run to Leeward except on the Full Moon I observed it ran very strong to Windward; I believe 'tis the same at change.

"May 22. Yesterday at 3 in the Afternoon we met with the Galleon under the East Island, but heard nothing of Mr. Hatley's Bark. At 9 last Night Jacob Scronder a Dutch-man and a very good Sailor, died. We kept on the Wind in the Morning to look under the Weather Island for Mr. Hatley, and fir'd a Gun for the Galleon to bear away for the Rendezvous Rock, which she did.

"May 23. Yesterday at 3 in the Afternoon we saw the Weather Island near enough, and no sail about it. We bore away in sight of the Rock, and saw none but our Galleon; we were in another Fright what became of our consort, and the 2 Prizes we left behind; but by 5 we saw' em come from under the Shore to the Leeward of the Rock. We spoke with 'em in the Evening; we all bewail'd Mr. Hatley and were afraid he was lost; We fir'd Guns all Night, and kept Lights out, in hopes he might see or hear us, and resolv'd to leave these unfortunate Islands, after we had viewed two or three more to Leeward. We pity'd our 5 Men in the Bark that is missing, who if in being have a melancholy Life without Water, having no more but for 2 Days, when they parted from us. Some are afraid they run on Rocks, and were lost in the Night, others that the 2 Prisoners and 3 Negroes had murder'd 'em when asleep; but if otherwise, we had no Water, and our Men being still sick, we could stay little longer for them. Last Night died Law Carney of a malignant Fever. There is hardly a Man in the Ship, who had been ashore at Guiaquil but has felt something of this Distemper, whereas not one of those that were not there have been sick yet. Finding that Punch did preserve my own Health I prescrib'd it freely among such of the Ship's Company as were well, to preserve theirs. Our Surgeons make heavy Complaints for want of sufficient Medecines, with till now I thought we abounded.

"May 21. Yesterday at 5 in the Afternoon we ran to the Northward and made another Island. . . and this Morning we sent our boat ashore, to see for the lost Bark, Water, Fish or Turtle. This Day Tho. Hughes a very good Sailor died, as did Mr. George Underhill, a good Proficient in most parts of the Mathematicks and other Learning, tho not much above 21 years old. He was of a very courteous Temper, and brave, was in the Fight where my Brother was kill'd, and serv'd as Lieutenant in my Company at Guiaquil. About the same time another young Man, call'd John English, died aboard the *Havre de Grace,* and we have many still sick...

"May 25. Yesterday at 6 in the Evening our Boat return'd from the Island without finding any Water, or seeing the Bark . . . Last Night Peter Marshal a good Sailor died. This morning our Boat with Mr. Selkirk's Bark went to another Island to view it . . .

"May 26. Last night our Boat and Bark return'd, haveing rounded the Island, found no Water but Plenty of Turtle and Fish. This Morning we joind'd the *Dutchess,* who had found no Water. About 12 a Clock we compar'd our Stocks of Water, found it absolutely necessary to make the best of our way to the Main for some, then to come off again ; and so much the rather, because we expected that 2 French Ships, one of 60, and another of 40 Guns, with some Spanish Men of War, would suddenly be in quest of us.

"May 30 . . . Had we supplied ourselves well at Point Arena, we should, no doubt, have had time enough to find the Island S. Maria de l'Aquada, reported to be one of the Gallapagos, where there is Plenty of good water, Timber, Land and Sea Turtle, and a Safe Road for Ships. . . Its probable there is such an Island, because once Capt. Davis, an Englishman, who was a buckaneering in these Seas, above 20 Years ago, lay some months and recruited here to Content; He says that it had Trees fit for Masts; but these sort of Men, and others I have convers'd with, or whose Books I have read, have given very blind or false Relations of their Navigation, and Actions in these Parts, for supposing the Places too remote to have their Stories disprov'd, they imposed on the Credulous, amongst whom I was one, till now I too plainly see that we cannot find any of their Relations to be relied on; Therefore I shall say no more of these Islands, since by what I saw of ' em, they don't at all answer the Description that those Men have given us".

" The *Duke* and the *Dutchess* returned to the mainland, and on September first set sail for the Galápagos again, where they spent almost two weeks searching for Hatley, the missing mate, his men and the inexplicably vanished ship. No trace of him was ever found though the rudder and "boltsprit" of a small bark lying on a beach led them to suppose at first that the mystery was explained. However, on examination these relics were found to be too old to be a part of the lost ship.' ' (1)

The buccaneers Courtney and Davis, with Dampier and Selkirk, returned to England in 1711 with booty that did not even cover the expenses of the Bristol merchants, which led to the termination of the agreements and contracts.

Alexander Selkirk returned without a shilling and wrote up his memoirs of those four years on the island in the Juan Fernández. Without much hope of getting them published, he showed them to a friend, who suggested that he show them to a writer, Daniel Defoe, who was becoming known. The writer kept the manuscript for some time and then returned it with a negative opinion of its worth. This discouraged Selkirk completely and he did not publish. A short time later Defoe's *Robinson Crusoe* appeared and was a tremendous success. Selkirk, however, died in poverty.

(1)   Beebe, W.: Galápagos: World's End, 1924 pág. 362.

What happened to Hatley and his ship which had disappeared in the Galapagos? A chance find on the other side of the world completes the story. A manuscript studied by the author in the Royal Navy Museum in Madrid in 1980 relates that Hatley reached the mainland after incredible suffering from lack of water and food. He and his crew were taken prisoners by the Spanish authorities and remained in prison until 1714, that is until after the war and the signing of the Treaty of Utrecht. Only then could they return to England.

Thus, the Archipelago became the almost obligatory retreat of bucaneers and pirates, especially once the principal sources of water had been located. The islands of Santa María de la Aguada (Floreana?) and Santiago were the most frequently visited, the first for water and tortoises and the second for the ample anchorages and the presence of water left by the winter rains. It was customary to sail for the islands after attacks on Spanish commerce, where the pirates could recuperate from combat, long voyages, and scanty rations.

In 1816 the expedition of Brown and Buchard against Guayaquil followed the same route. The first named took on 70 tortoisses before sailing for Buenos Aires.

ADDITIONAL READINGS:

Rose, Ruth: "The man and the Galapagos,'' in Beebe, W.: "Galápagos: World's End", New York, 1924.

Larrea, Carlos M. "El Archipiélago de Colón (Galápagos)". Casa de la Cultura Ecuatoriana, Quito, 1960.

Estrada Ycaza, Julio: "El Puerto de Guayaquil", Tomo I. Guayaquil, 1972.

Bernal Ruiz, María del Pilar: "La Toma del Puerto de Guayaquil en 1687", Sevilla, 1979.

LARGE SPANISH SHIP OF THE 18th CENTURY

LARGE SPANISH SHIP OF THE 13TH CENTURY

CHAPTER III

AN IRISH EMPEROR IN THE GALAPAGOS

The English and Dutch corsairs used to abandon rebelious sailors and other undesirable persons from their ships on islands, among them the Galapagos. Due to the lack of water on most islands, a sailor abandoned there could consider himself dead.

On the other hand, the ship's arrival in the Galapagos Islands must not have been a totally pleasant experience for the crews. They arrived with their last rations of water and the hated biscuit which was their everyday fare. Even for the well—behaved sailors who had nothing to fear from their captains, the stay meant hard work locating the few sources of water and then transporting it to the beach in unconfortable vessels. The descriptions of endless collection of water which had to be carried great distances over a terrain covered with lava, rocks and cactus, reflected the dislike they must have felt for that indispensable task. Besides, they did not always encounter good water, especially when they were unable to locate springs and had to be satisfied with rainwater accumulations left over from the previous winter.

The job of obtaining food provisions was easier because of the abundant tortoises and fish. But, even so, transporting animals that weighed 200 pounds over rocky and hilly terrain was not easy, as described by Dampier.

The visitors' first impression when they discovered the unagresive tortoises was an agreeable surprise and they turned them over so they could not run away. Later on they realized that the heavy tortoises not only did not run away but were present everywhere. While they were in the islands, it was an easy matter to send the cook onto land to kill and prepare as many tortoises as desired. Those that were carried on board were destined for the food stores. How many tortoises were killed during two centuries of visits by the pirates, the English and North American whalers?. It is hard to tell. Estimates based on the journals of whaling ships in the past century bring the calculation to several hundred thou - sand. And what about those that were never registred in the jour- nals or were killed on land?

Securing other provisions, especilly vegetables, was not possi- ble. Despite this, the tired seamen searched for any plant, such as wild fruits, herbs, etc., that could add to, or at least vary, their re- petitious fare during the coming months.

Colnet's discovery, in 1793, of a plant that could be substitu- ted for the good chinese tea is interesting. He wrote: "The earth produces wild mint, sorrel and a plant resembling the cloth—tree of Otaheite and the Sandwich Isles, whose leaves are an excellent substitute for the China tea, and was indeed preferred to it by my people as well as by myself".

Thus the visits of the English and Dutch corsairs and the North American whalers had concrete objectives: water, fish and tortoises, to which we can add a few birds, especially doves, which were easily caught.

Finding a cultivated field on the islands could easily be consi- dered a hallucination. But that occurred at the beginning of the nineteenth century when a strange Irishman who had proclaimed himself "emperor", was discovered on Charles Island (Floreana)

When the North American, Captain William Porter, stopped at the Galapagos Islands in 1812 during the war against England, he encountered the recent story of this curious personage which he retold in all of its details.

". . . on the east side of the island (Charles) there is another landing, which he calls Pat's landing; and this place will probably immortalize an Irish man, named Patrick Watkins, who some years since he an English ship, and took up his abode on this island, and built himself a miserable hut, about a mile from the landing called after him, in a valley containing about two acres of ground capable of cultivation, and perhaps the only spot on the island which affords sufficient moisture for the purpose. Here he succeeded in raising potatoes and pumpkins in considerable quantities, which he generally exchanged for rum, or sold for cash. The appearance of this man, from the accounts I have received of him, was the most dreadful that can be imagined; ragged clothes, scarce sufficient to cover his nakedness, and covered with vermin; his red hair and beard matted, his skin much burnt, from constant exposure to the sun, and so wild and savage in his manner and appearance, that he struck everyone with horror. For several years this wretched being lived by himself on this desolate spot, without any apparent desire than that of procuring rum in sufficient quantities to keep himself intoxicated, and, at such times, after an absence from his hut of several days, he would be found in a state of perfect insensibility, rolling among the rocks of the mountains. He appeared to be reduced to the lowest grade of which human nature is capable, and seemed to have no desire beyond the tortoises and other animals of the island, except that of getting drunk. But this man, wretched and miserable as he may have appeared, was neither destitute of ambition, nor incapable of undertaking an enterprise that would have appalled the heart of any other man; nor was he devoid of the talent of rousing others to second his hardihood.

"He by some means became possessed of an old musket, and a few charges of powder and ball; and the possession of this weapon probably first stimulated his ambition. He felt himself strong as the sovereing of the island, and was desirous of proving his strength on the first human being that fell in his way, which happened to be a negro, who was left in charge of a boat belonging to an American ship that had touched there for refreshments. Patrick came down to the beach where the boat lay, armed with his musket, now become his constant companion, directed the negro, in an authoritative manner, to follow him, and on his refusal, snapped his musket at him twice, which luckily missed fire. The negro, however, became intimidated, and followed him. Patrick now shouldered his musket, marched off before, and on his way up the mountain exultingly informed the negro he was henceforth to work for him, and become his slave, and that his good or bad treatment would depend on his future conduct. On arriving at a narrow defile and perceiving Patrick off his guard, the negro seized the moment, grasped him in his arms, threw him down, tied his arms behind, shouldered him, and carried him to his boat, and when the crew had arrived he was taken on board the ship. An English smuggler was lying in the harbour at the same time, the captain of which sentenced Patrick to be severely whipped on board both vessels, which was put in execution, and he was afterward taken on shore handcuffed by the Englishmen, who compelled him to make known where he had concealed the few dolars he had been enabled to accumulate from the sale of his potatoes and pumpkins, which they took from him. But while they were busy in destroying his hut and garden, the wretched being made his escape, and concealed himself among the rocks in the interior of the island, until the ship had sailed, when he ventured from his hiding–place, and by means of an old file, which he drove into a tree, freed himself from the handcuffs. He now meditated a severe revenge, but concealed his intentions. Vessels continued to touch there, and Patrick, as usual, to furnish them with vegetables; but from time to time he was enabled, by administering potent draughts of his darling liquor to some of the men of the crews, and getting them so drunk that they were rendered insensible, to conceal them until the ship had sailed; when, finding themselves entirely dependent on him, they willingly enlisted under his banners, became his slaves, and he the most absolute of of tyrants. By this means he had augmented the number to five, including himself, and every means was used by him to endeavour to procure arms for them, but without effect. It is supposed that his object was to have surprised some vessel, massacred her crew, and taken her off. While Patrick was meditating his plans, two ships, an American and an English vessel, touched there and applied to Patrick for vegetables. He promised them the greatest abundance, provided they would send their boats to his landing, and their people to bring them from his garden, informing them that his rascals had become so indolent of late, that he could not get them to work. This arrangement was agreed to; two boats were sent from each vessel and hauled on the beach. Their crews all went to Patrick's habitation, but neither he nor any of his people were to be found; and, after waiting until their patience was exhausted, they returned to the beach, where they found only the wreck of three of their boats, which were broken to pieces and the fourth one missing. They succeeded, however, after much difficulty, in getting around to the bay apposite to their ships, where other boats were sent to their relief; and the commanders of the ships, apprehensive of some other trick, saw no security except in a flight from the island, leaving Patrick and his gang in quiet possession of the boat. But before they sailed, they put a letter in a keg, giving intelligence of the affair, and moored it in the bay, where it was found by Captain Randall, but not until he had sent his boat to Patrick's landing, for the purpose of procuring refreshments; and, as may be easily supposed, he felt no little inquietude until her return, when she brought him a letter from Patrick to the following purport, which was found in his hut.

— "SIR,

"I have made repeated applications to captains of vessels to sell me a boat, or to take me from this place, but in every instance met with a refusal. An opportunity presented itself to possess myself of one, and I took advantage of it. I have been a long time endeavouring, by hard labour and suffering, to accumulate wherewithal to make myself comfortable; but at different times have been robbed and maltreated, and in a late instance by captain Paddock, whose conduct in punishing me and robbing me of about five hundred dollars, in cash and other articles, neither agrees with the principles he professes, nor is it such as his sleek coat would lead one to expect(1).

"On the 29th of March, 1809, I sail from the enchanted island in the *Black Prince*, bound to the Marquesas.

"Do not kill the old hen; she is now sitting and will soon

---

1 Captain Paddock was of the Society of Friends.

have chicks.

(Signed)   FATHERLESS OBERLUS."

"Patrick arrived alone at Guayaquil in his open boat, the rest who sailed with him having perished for want of water, or, as is generally supposed, were put to death by him on his finding the water to grow scarce. From thence he proceeded to Payta, where he wound himself into the affection of a tawny damsel, and prevailed on her to consent to accompany him back to his enchanted island, the beauties of which he no doubt painted in glowing colours; but, from his savage appearance, he was there considered by the police as a suspicious person, and being found under the keel of a small vessel then ready to be launched, and suspected of some improper intention, he was confined in Payta gaol, where he now remains, and probably owing to this circumstance Charles Island, as well as the rest of the Gallipagos, may remain unpopulated for many ages to come. This reflection may naturally lead us to a consideration of the question concerning the population of the other islands scattered about the Pacific ocean, respecting which so many conjectures have been hazarded. I shall only hazard one, which is briefly this; that former ages may have produced men equally as bold and daring as Pat, and women as willing as his fair one to accompany them on their adventurous voyages. And when we consider the issue which might be produced from a union between a red—haired wild Irishman and a copper—coloured mixt—blooded squaw, we need not be any longer surprised at the different varieties in human nature.

"If Patrick should be liberated from durance, and arrive with his love at this enchanting spot, perhaps (when neither he nor the Gallipagos are any longer remembered) some future navigator may surprise the world by a discovery of them, and his accounts of the strange people with which they may probably be inhabited".

CHAPTER IV

THE FIRST COLONY ENDS IN BLOODSHED

If anyone wanted to claim credit for the name of the Archipe - lago or some of the islands of the Galapagos, Don José de Villamil would have the most right . He was born in Louisiana of a Spanish father and a French mother and came to Guayaquil on business in 1811. Villamil settled in that city and participated in the struggles of the new republic until his death in 1866.

Although they belonged to Spain and had been visited and explored several times during the 17th and 18th centuries, the Galapagos Islands had never been settled nor were they considered in the division of the political jurisdiction of the viceroyalties. On some maps they appear as part of the Royal Audiencia of Quito, but after Independence they were a no-man's land.

José de Villamil convinced the Goverment of Ecuador, which had come into existence in 1830, that it should annex the Archipelago. It was incorporated into the new republic officially and with solemnity on February 12th 1832 in a ceremony presided over by Colonel Ignacio Hernández, the government delegate, on the island called Floreana at the time in honor of President Juan J. Flores. Present were the ship's crew, a group of colonists, and a complement of foreigners from a whaling ship who were invited as witnesses.

Villamil was not content to assist in the annexation of the islands; he was thinking of a full-scale colonization scheme. The first group of colonists which attended the ceremony of annexation was the vanguard of his grand plan. Villamil himsel arrived on the 19th of the same month to personally oversee the first steps of the new colony.

He selected the best area for the beginning of the colony, which he called "Asilo de la Paz" or Haven of Peace, next to the spring a few kilometers from Black Beach (Playa Prieta). He distributed parcels of land around the spring.

In October of 1832, Villamil was named Governor of Galapagos. As such he established himself on the island in order to organize and encourage the project in person. He established clear and humane rules which were to govern the new colony: all were free to act and work, but they were required to contribute to community work such as building roads and a system to bring water.

Unfortunately the Governor made two mistakes which in the end were to destroy the colony: the inclusion of convicts and the choice of city-dwellers. The first group of colonists was made up of the mutinous soldiers from the Flores Batallion who had been condemned to death. Villamil interceded on their behalf and obtained the commutation of their sentence to exile in the Galapagos. In the following years other persons in trouble with the law arrived, ladies of easy virtue, vagabonds, and debtors, all of whom had a negative impact on the colonists.

The second error mentioned, the selection of city-dwellers, was also decisive. The French traveller, Du Petit Thouars, who visited the colony in 1838 left us his impressions of the population. The inhabitants were very hospitable and even in their poverty did not hesitate to offer the new arrivals the produce of their gardens: vegetables, fruit and milk; but they were anxious to return to the mainland as soon as possible. To their longing for the bustle and sound of the city was added their distress at living among persons of ill repute. Villamil took advantage of every journey to Guayaquil to recruit artisans and workers, but in a short time all lost their enthusiasm and longed for the distant life of the city. They were not accustomed to the loneliness of the country.

The Governor tried to encourage stockraising and his partner, Captain Lawson brought out all kinds of domestic animals: cattle, horses, sheep and pigs. All of these animals flourished in the islands.

Captain Lawson replaced Villamil in 1835 during the civil war in which two of his friends, Juan J. Flores and Vicente Rocafuerte led the rival factions. The civil war also brought about new deportations of condemned soldiers. In 1838, Du Petit Thouars, the French traveller already cited, noted that the population living in there was about 300 persons of whom 150 were political prisoners, although their actions indicated less political convictions than violent attitudes. No doubt they were dangerous adventurers who became soldiers to try their fortune. (1)

Charles Darwin stopped at the island in 1835 as well and described it as follows:

"The houses are scattered over the cultivated ground and form what would be called a 'Pueblo' (village) . . . It appears that the people are far from contented, they complain here of the deficiency of money: I presume there is some more essential want than that of mere currency, namely want of sale of their produce. . . The inhabitants here lead a sort of Robinson Crusoe life; the houses are very simple, built of poles and thatched with grass. Part of their time is employed in hunting the wild pigs and goats with which the woods abound; from the climate agriculture requires but a small portion. The main article is the Terrapin or Tortoise; such numbers yet remain, that is calculated two days' hunting will find food for the other five days in the week . . ."

Villamil resigned as Governor in 1837 and the following year an Englishman, Colonel J. Williams, was named in his place. He soon became notorious for his cruelty. This English soldier did not disguise his contempt and mistrust of the creoles. Williams surrounded himself with foreigners from the whaling ships, whom he convinced with promises and made overseers with the power to punish and even kill the Ecuadorean workers. Backed up by such men, Williams initiated a reign of terror among the colonists who were forced to work without rest and without any recompense other than poor food.

1.— Judde, Gabriel: "Les Isles Galapagos vues par trois voyageurs Francais: N. Vaillant, A.A. Dupetit Thouars et A. Charton" p. 580.

DON JOSE DE VILLAMIL

First Promoter of the colonization of the Galapagos after the anexation of the islands by Ecuador in 1832.

General Mena, who had remained as Villamil's representative, was sickened at so much injustice and brutality and left the island to seek refuge on Chatham Island.

The period from 1839 to 1841 was perhaps the bitterest for the colonists; the growing brutality of Williams and his overseers were responsible for the rage of the colonists and former soldiers who awaited an opportunity to take revenge for so much punishment and humiliation. Williams and his overseers knew that the situation could not last, despite their strict vigilance and cruel punishments. The foreigners did not understand the secrets of the Spanish language and the colonists prepared their uprising using veiled language. One day the 200 inhabitants of the island made common cause and, armed with sticks, machetes, stones and garrotes, they attacked the foreigners and forced them to flee. Williams had a ship ready in the harbor on which he embarked to save his skin and disappeared from the Galapagos.

Villamil found out about these events some time afterward and left for the islands to salvage his project. It was too late. Many had already left the island and the 80 persons remaining sought to return to the mainland by any means. Villamil, seeing that the colony was breaking up, decided on the only possible solution: he took the few colonists whom he could convince to stay in the Galapagos to Chatham and also took there all the livestock he could. The rest he left free on the islands of Floreana and Isabela. These animals multiplied in large numbers, though to a lesser extent on Floreana where feral dogs killed many of the newborn. Villamil returned to the mainland broken -hearted.

There were 25 convicts living on Floreana in 1845 since the government continued to use the island as a penal colony for the most dangerous criminals. That same year Villamil was named Commander General of the Guayas District and he tried to send some colonists to the Islands. Two years later in 1847 he sought permission to organize a new colony, but the situation in the country and the attempts of the former president Flores, to invade Ecuador did not allow Villamil to devote more time to this project.

The French traveller Charton passed through the islands in 1848 and found some 90 exiles, for the most part soldiers, who called themselves political prisoners. They lived in 12 tumbledown houses without the least desire to work; they only wanted to escape from the island to continue their misdeeds.

By 1850 the presence of Ecuador in the islands was nominal, precisely at a time when several western powers discovered the strategic and commercial value of the Archipelago. Belatedly, they had realized that the desolate islands, in spite of their distance from the mainland, could serve as a strategic base and possibly as a stopping place for traders. Unfortunately the Ecuadorian administrations gave no thought to the islands except as a prison for the worst criminals.

In 1851 a group of prisoners managed to seize a launch and set out to sea; they were never heard of again.

The political situation in Ecuador darkend once again in 1852 because of the renewed threats of an invasion by former president Juan José Flores. Shortly before a famous criminal with the surname Briones had arrived on Floreana. He was known as the "Pirate of the Guayas" because of his clever attacks. To Briones and his companions the news of the great confusion caused by the imminent invasion by Flores seemed to offer a fine opportunity for escape, since all of the military garrison had been returned to the mainland.

At the end of 1852 the American whaling ship George Howland anchored off Floreana and, as was customary, the captain and four crewmen landed to provision the boat with water and tortoise meat. Briones and his men, who had been lying in wait, fell on them and captured the whalers. Another boat with eight men on board followed and met the same fate. Only six crewmen remained on the whaling ship and these had to surrender. The crew was left on the island while Briones and his men sailed to Chatham, the seat of the territorial government. The Governor, Mena, was captured and the farm on the island were sacked. Briones then sailed for the mainland. The Governor was brutally murdered at sea and his body thrown to the sharks.

The intentions of Briones were unclear; he probably intended to continue his life of crime in the Gulf of Guayaquil, however, it happened that as his ship entered the Gulf, two small sloops, which were the vanguard of General Flores's invasion force, were seen as they sailed to their rendevous at Puná Island. The sloops were full of unarmed recruits who gazed indifferently at the approaching American whaler.

Briones went off in a boat with eight of his companions and ordered the first sloop to stop. Suspecting nothing, the sloops lost ways as the pirates, with their knives and machetes hidden, manoeuvered to put the sloops in line. Suddenly Briones shouted and the eight fell on the defenseless recruits machete in hand. Arms and heads rolled on the deck before they knew what was happening. When the recruits tried to defend themselves, it was already too late; each pirate had killed two or three and the survivors could only beg for mercy. Briones spared no one. After this bloodbath the bodies of 20 men and their officer, Tamayo, lay on the sloop's decks.

With a smile of triumph, Briones called on his men to attack the second sloop which was desperately trying to flee this scene of horror. The sloop was heavy, but was fighting for its life. The pirates rowed furiously since they knew that if the men on the sloop escaped, they would be their accusers. In desperation, the sloop was run ashore on Puná Island and the men hid in the mangrove. Briones and his men could not overtake them although some attemped pursuit. The leader returned to the sloop with the men he could round up and, abandoning the whaler, sailed for Guayaquil where they expected to be received as heroes because they had destroyed the vanguard of General Flores's invasion.

However, they received a cold welcome since the memory of their attacks was fresh. Opportune help had come from an unwanted quarter. The authorities soon learned what had happened from the mouths of other prisoners and the fugitives. Definitely this providential ally could not be counted as a friend. Briones and his men were taken prisoner, despite their protests, summarily sentenced and executed. The defense of the nation could not condone such blood—thirsty monsters.

The Briones incident gave rise to bothersome international problems: the return of the whaler, which was taken as a prize by a foreign vessel after being abandoned in the Gulf, and whose owner Matthew Holland claimed damages of $ 40.000,oo through the United States Chargé d'Affaires in Guayaquil.

These two problems were settled happily without major expense, but in the process the international interest in acquiring or leasing of the Galapagos became clear. The United States Chargé d'Affaires wrote to his goverment to the effect that surely Ecuador, in view of its incapacity to guard the islands which provided no revenue to the treasury, would be disposed to cede them under favorable circumstances. England, on the other hand, sought a concession of at least one island. These pressures increased as rumors of the presence of large amounts of guano on the islands began to spread.

Meanwhile Floreana Island had again been filled with prisoners and exiles who aroused concern among visitors to the place. The following year, 1853, the Ecuadorean schooner, *Azuay*, commanded by Captain Gurney, fell into a trap. Two groups of sailors were seized by the prisoners who demanded a boat capable of sailing to the mainland in exchange for the men. Captain Gurney asked for time and sailed to Chatham for weapons and more men. When he returned to Floreana, he had a plan, which was not discovered by the mutineers. He anchored off Post Office, but landed boatloads of armed men at Playa Prieta where the convicts awaited them. Gurney approached them and demanded the return of his men. When this was refused, he attacked and set fire to the nearest house. The captive men from the schooner took advantage of the confusion to escape to Post Office where they picked up by Gurney's men.

1854 was marked by intense international pressure to obtain concessions for the exploitation of guano, based on reports by the financier, Jules Brissot, who specified neither the location nor the quantity involved.

Philo While, the United States envoy resident in Quito, applied even more pressure on the basis of Brissot's statements until, in September, the steamer, *Guayas,* sailed with Villamil and three North Americans (Captain Game, Mr. Washburn and Mr. Smyrk) on a mission to clear up the matter once and for all. This voyage is described in Villamil's diary in which he describes with a note of frustration the trip to all the corners of the islands where they had been assured there were large quantities of guano. In spite of the disappointing results, a contract for the exploitation of guano was signed but it lapsed the following year because the foreign firms did not meet its stipulations. (1) Interest in guano was replaced by the discovery of archil , a lichen used in dyes, which aroused the ambition of several Guayaquil businessmen.

Villamil, meanwhile, had not abandoned his project to exploit the resources of the islands. This time he wanted to exploit the feral livestock on Albemarle and Chatham. He formed a company with several North Americans for the extraction of tallow which only lasted a few years because of the difficulties of distance, lack of workers and technical facilities.

Unquestionably, Villamil was not a man who gave up his dreams easily. Shortly afterward he founded the Empresa Agrícola y Pecuaria de Chatham (Chatham Agricultural and Livestock Company) with an adventurer named Norton. When it seemed that Villamil's efforts were finally going to bear fruit, a schooner commanded by a Captain Fernandez arrived one day to investigate certain previous "miracles" of Norton's, who was famous as a healer. Norton was taken prisoner and, in the course of the crossing, for unknown reasons, Captain Fernandez had him shot.

At last, Villamil gave up. He had exhausted his capital without obtaining any return and now his health began to fail with age. In 1860 he sold part of his rights to Floreana Island to a French adventurer named Leon Ithurburu, to whom he owed money for several loans. Ithurburu wanted to search for pirates' treasure and

(1).— Villamil, José: "Diario del viaje de exploración a Galápagos", Archivo Nacional de Historia, Quito, Min. Interior, Gobernación de Guayaquil, 1954.

sunken ships, about which legends had grown up. He shipped out "pneumatic" equipment and diving suits, but in vain. Two years later this curious equipment was offered for sale.

Villamil died in 1866 and with him ended the first attempt to colonize the islands. His tenacity was not enough and the only tangible result was the increase in the numbers of erstwhile domestic animals on several islands which served as an incentive for other adventurers.

The curse of the tortoise was fulfilled once again: every attempt to exploit the islands at the expense of their enviroment would end in failure or death.

The experiences of this extraordinary man were not heeded nor were his errors corrected. Those who came after him followed in the same path. They attempted to work with ex-convicts and after a period of apparent success, they ended paying for their mistakes with their lives.

Epilogue

The cession of part of Floreana Island to Leon Ithurburu had unexpected consequences. When he died, Ithurburu willed his rights to the Office of Welfare of the commune of Bacus in the French Pyrenees. Thirty years later in 1884, the French government sought a concession in the Galapagos with the pretext of "protecting the rights of its citizens", but in fact to obtain a strategic location with the opening of the Panama Canal in mind. The negotiations were long and difficult until the French government finally recognized Ecuadorean sovereignty over the islands in 1887. This decision was influenced by pressure from the United States to obtain for that country the rental or sale of all or part of the Archipelago.

In 1951, presumed descendents of Ithurburu made another claim for the rights to the island of Floreana of the commune of

Bacus, which at the time had 1.200 inhabitants. Once again papers and documents were studied to clarify the matter. The conclusions reached may be summarized as follows: in the first place, only part of the island had been ceded, not the whole thing. In the second place, private ownership did not affect national sovereignty. Finally, the claimants had not recognized that almost a century had passed in the course of which legislation was passed on more than one occasion requiring owners to bring their titles up to date on pain of loss if they did not comply.

What the great powers were unable to obtain was almost achieved by a French Basque. The world lost the opportunity to visit a Basque enclave in the Galapagos!

ADDITIONAL READINGS:

Larrea, Carlos M. "El Archipiélago de Colón", Quito, 1960
Slevin, J. R. "The Galapagos Islands. A history of their exploration", 1959.

CHARLES ISLAND (FLOREANA) View by Darwin in 1833

CHAPTER V

INNOCENT BLOOD ON FLOREANA.
THE MURDER OF JOSE VALDIZAN. 1878

Of all the crimes committed on the Galapagos, the murder of Jose Valdizan is without a doubt the most unjust and irrational of them all. Don Jose Valdizan was a Spanish gentleman who had lived in Ecuador for many years and was married to Carmen Rubira, a lady from Guayaquil. He was very experienced in agriculture and felt a great attraction for the Galapagos Islands. After arranging his permits with the Villamil family, owners of most of Floreana, he enthusiastically set off for the islands.

In 1869, he won the exclusive rights to "mine" archil, a lichen highly sought after in the dyeing industry. He was without competitors as Don Manuel J. Cobos had dropped out of the bidding because of problems with Gabriel Garcia Moreno's government. Don Jose came to reside on the island with his family and organized a cattle and agricultural ranch with a large group of work ers who were to become a type of extended family similar to the biblical patriarchs. He was kind to the extreme and was convinced that even goodness could change the most wicked wrongdoer.

He committed one error which would later prove fatal: accepting a growing number of prisoners from the jails of Guayaquil whom he hoped to convert into citizens who would be both useful and beneficial to the nation. He refused to listen to the advice of his friends and little by little took on as workers icreasing numbers of prisoners. He won some of them over through his kindness, one of whom was Anatolio Lindao who became his trusted assistant. Don Jose was after all not totally naive and in spite of his goodwill, his foremen were told to keep a strict watch over the forced laborers.

During the next eight years, Don Jose was able to expand the

DON JOSE VALDIZAN

A Spanish gentleman murdered on Floreana in 1878

lands under cultivation to the upper plateaus on the island to such an extent that he was able to maintain regular trade with Guayaquil using his own boats. At the same time he took advantage of the products that the other islands had to offer such as archil and turtle oil which were used for the street lighting in the cities on the coast.

At the beginning of 1878 we find Don Jose with his wife in Guayaquil making his annual trip to visit relatives and deal with business affairs. By mid March, his schooner "Venecia" was ready to set sail to the Galapagos with a large number of prisoners on board. Don Jose had ignored once again the advice of his friends who did not approve of mixing honest workers with the undesir - ables from the jails. Among these prisoners were Lucas Alvarado, Pablo Mendez, Teofilo Mendez, José Galindo and others.

One of the honest workers was Jose Federico Salazar, a ship's carpenter in charge of maintaining and restoring the sloops·and ships, an important job as the conditions on the Galapagos re- quired maintaining the vessels in the best possible shape.

The "Venecia", under the command of Captain Nicolas Petersen, set sail from Guayaquil at the beginning of May , stopping in Chanduy to pick up some workers and then in the vi- llage of Ballenita, on the Santa Elena peninsula, where Carmen Rubira waited with her friend Zoila Enriquez.

The schooner "Venecia" was a very sea—worthy ship and in four days, they arrived on Floreana Island. Upon approaching Black Beach, they saw a crowd of workers with their families and foremen who had come to welcome them and receive their mail and packages from Guayaquil. Don Jose was very concerned about the welfare of his workers and in his trips to the mainland, spent many days visiting their families and always agreed to bring back to Floreana whatever was requested of him.

On the beach they could see the Englishman Thomas Levick, the ranch supervisor, who had decided to work for Don Jose on Floreana when his wife died. Also present was the faithful and unfailing foreman Jose Aragon as well as Manuel Pesantez and Catalino Catuto and others.

Upon landing, everyone approached Don Jose and gave him the customary greeting, an embrace, especially his nephew Macario Diaz, an adolescent who thought of Don José as his own father. He had as a friend another boy, Bernardo Pozo, Dona Carmen's servant.

After unloading countless bundles, the march to the ranch, which was many kilometers inland from the coast, was organized. The first ones to take a load were the prisoners who looked on everyone with hate and resentment in contrast with the happiness and spontaneity of the workers. Only Jose Federico Salazar and the prisoner Jose Galindo spent the night in the huts on the beach in order to inspect the ship before its trip to Isabella Island where it would load up with oil to take to Guayaquil.

The next day, everyone assembled for work, payment of their wages, and assignment of new jobs. Captain Levick with 60 men would take charge of the land under cultivation, while the foreman Jose Aragon, with 36 men, would enlarge the pasture grounds to increase cattle production.

The presence of the patriarch Don Jose infused the population with new spirit. But the recently arrived criminals were only to feel hate and envy, as they felt trapped out in middle of the ocean and ultimately they could not resign themselves to live an ordinary life. Soon several of whom wished to return to their old tricks on the mainland, united under the common cause of escape. Among them was the previously mentioned Anatolio Lindao whom Don Jose had treated with special deference in the hope of saving a "lost sheep."

Anatolio Lindao's house became the center of the conspiracy because he assured the least suspicion and he seemed to attract the most violent ones, such as Alvarado, Martinez, Mendez and others, who all congregated there. The ranch house was located at "Refuge of Peace", some 8 kilometers from the beach, surrounded, albeit at some distance, by the workers' homes. The convicts had their communal huts somewhat farther away and watch was kept on them.

No one realized there was a conspiracy afoot because they

could see no reason for such an undertaking given the distance from the mainland, the small number of prisoners in relation to the numbers of faithful workers, and above all, Don Jose's kindness. Nonetheless, the conspiracy was under way and the date for the coup was set for the middle of July as they suspected that around that time one of the sailing ships would arrive which would be able to take them to the mainland.

Don Jose's house was a two—story structure with a terrace and surrounded by an extensive garden filled with flowers thanks to Carmen Rubira's dedication. While the workers were in the fields, the cook, Eusebio Quimi, Doña Carmen's servant, Bernardo Pozo, and an occasional worker in charge of the neighboring garden alone remained at the house. The foreman Jose Aragon, nevertheless, was in the habit of patrolling nearby in case of any attack as he had realized how unhappy the newly arrived criminals were.

Unfortunately, his caution was well advised because one day in July of 1878, Jose Aragon was returning from inspecting the work in the fields when in the bend of the road, he was attacked by Mendez and Peña with a machete. Thinking he was dead, the two men dragged him off into the bushes to hide their crime. They then met up with Alvarado and headed towards their employer's house, who was surprised to see them away from their jobs. They pretended they were coming to ask his permission to have the day off. Don Jose refused permission in his usual courteous manner, giving them very good reasons, and endeavored to convince them of the value of an honest day's work. The criminals pretended to listen but in reality were waiting for the opportune moment to commit the crime. Don Jose wanted to show them that he sympathized and offered them a drink. He spent a moment with them and they then left. A minute later Alvarado returned because he had liked the drink so much and asked for another. Don Jose consented but when he bent down to put the bottle behind his desk, the criminal stabbed him on the left side with an enormous dagger and ran to meet his fellow conspirators. The conspirators, who numbered 15, then set out to liquidate all nearby loyal workers.

Don Jose was able to drag himself inside the house and alert his wife and Eusebio Quimi, who nursed him the best he could. After Eusebio tied a band of cloth around the injury to keep the intestines in place, they both headed towards the garden where they could hide from the criminals who would surely return. Doña Carmen had left before to go to get help but had gotten lost in the thick underbrush. Eusebio went after her but when he could not find her and therefore headed towards the fields to warn Thomas Levick and the other laborers. Unfortunately, the road was long and winding and he did not arrive until a couple of hours later.

In order to carry out their plans, the criminals had divided themselves into two groups. Anatolio Lindao and another ran to the garden where Bernardo Pozo was working and before he even realized it, they decapitated him with a machete. Mendez and Peña headed towards the port to kill Federico Salazar but they arrived too late as Macario Diaz, Don Jose's nephew who had seen the crime from a distance, alerted him and together they took a short-cut to the ranch. They thought it strange the way Don Jose's assistant, Galindo, reacted but said nothing. Macario Diaz left to warn another group of workers who were near Post Office.

Salazar was approaching the ranch house when he was surrounded and fired on by a group of criminals, but they missed because he was able to throw himself to the ground in time. Nonetheless he was captured and they dragged him to the house where almost all of the conspirators had gathered and tied him to a pillar so he would be forced to witness the party that was beginning.

Practically everyone was there. They had sacked the house and were ready to celebrate their triumph with the liquor that Don Jose had brought from Guayaquil. For a few moments they discussed whether or not to kill Salazar but they finally decided to spare him so he could navigate the ship back to the mainland.

Alvarado and Martinez, the most bood—thirsty of them all,

armed with a carbine set out to kill some laborers who were working a ways away. Two of these laborers had heard the shots and armed with machetes, returned home to see what had happened. The two were known by their nicknames, the first called "Seis Reales", because he had six fingers on one hand, and the other "Guapuro", because of his habit of drinking hard cane alcohol mixed with water. In a turn in the road, they came across the outlaws. Alvarado shot point blank but the gun didn't fire. " Six Reales" brandished his machete and with one single blow, cracked the criminal's skull while "Guapuro" finished him off with a blow with a stone. Valdizan's assassin then was to die before his victim. Martinez, frightened by what he had seen, returned to the ranch to warn his buddies, but they paid no attention to him as they were right in the middle of a party, tipsy from all the liquor and confident with the weapons on hand.

It was in the middle of the afternoon as they were just getting ready to go hide out in the hills and wait for the arrival of the ship, when they heard some steps in the garden.

Eusebio Quimi had alerted Thomas Levick and he in turn organized his men, all of whom headed towards the ranch with the intention of making the criminals pay dearly for their crime. Levick had a brand new carbine and as he was a fan of hunting cattle on horseback, hoped that he equally successful with these human beasts who had so vilely murdered his boss. Everyone was especially furious with Lindao, who after having received so many signs of Don Jose's confidence, had betrayed him. Levick's men moved to close off the escape route to the outlaws, whose cries and shouts could be heard from far away.

Merchan and Galindo looked out on the terrace to see what all the noise was in the garden. Levick carefully aimed at and shot the former who gave a jump and fell to the garden. Upon hearing the shot, another outlaw stuck his head out the window. Levick quickly saw him as well as another drunk who was trying to fire on him and he despatched them both. Galindo seeing that all was lost and tried to escape by the back door but Catalino Catuto chased him down and killed him with one machete blow to the head. Levick continued to fire without wasting a single bullet.

When there were no more signs of life, they entered the house where they found twelve bodies. They freed Salazar and moved Don Jose's lifeless body. The only ones missing were Martinez and Lindao who had left the house a little earlier and had not returned. One group set out to find them while another searched for Doña Carmen who was also missing.

Federico Salazar located the badly injured Aragon and with the help of some other workers he was moved home. He was in bad shape but his wounds were not fatal. By nightfall, Martinez was found and taken to the ranch where he was tied to a stake. More than one wanted to finish him off but Levick was opposed: they could not follow the example set by the criminals especially given the fact that Martinez was injured.

The search party organized to find Doña Carmen turned up a trace which made everyone even more worried as they feared the worst.

Don Jose's body was placed in the living room, and the carpenter Federico Salazar took charge of building the coffin in as short a time as possible. The laborers held the wake all night, mourning Dona Carmen's absence.

The next day the coffin was finished and in the midst of everyone's distress, Don Jose was buried in the garden a few yards from the house. The day before, the criminal's bodies had been buried in a common grave at some distance from the house. A more extensive search was organized for Doña Carmen, with no results. On the third day she was found in terrible condition with her dress and legs destroyed by the undergrowth, severely weakened by lack of food and water. She was taken home where she was nursed with great tenderness. When she recovered, she dedicated herself to taking care of poor Aragon who was still very ill.

Cap. Thomas Levick, 83, was still alive in San Cristobal Is in 1926.

(Stein Hoff: Drommem om Galapagos, 1985, p.39))

In a litter made of branches, he was brought to the ranch house where he fully recovered under Doña Carmen's care. The wicked Lindao was not found even though they searched all over the island for him.

Two weeks later small schooner, "Santa Elena" arrived under the command of Captain Leonidas Drouet and anchored at Black Beach. A couple of days later, the boatswain went down into the hold of the ship and noticed a sudden movement. It was the outlaw Lindao who had slipped on board during the night. He was caught and confessed his crimes, especially the vicious murder of poor Bernardo Pozo.

On August 22, 1878 the schooner set sail for Guayaquil taking Doña Carmen and the murderers who were to be tried in Guayaquil. Thomas Levick remained on the island to take care of ranch business. None of the workers wanted to remain on the accursed island and they waited for the next boat that would take them anywhere off the island. Many decided to move to Chatham Island where Manuel J. Cobos and José Monroy, recently arrived from México, had begun to work. Among those that went to Chatham were Jose Salazar, Eusebio Quimí , and a couple of years later, Thomas Levick. These names were to figure in the history of Chatham at the turn of the century. Federico Salazar was to build the coffins for Manuel J. Cobos and Leonardo Reyna, assassinated on Chatham Island in January of 1904. And so ended this new attempt to colonize Floreana which seemed condemned to tragedy. The cultivated fields and the cattle so well kept by Valdizán were abandoned. But as later reports tell us, they remained as a mystery and a source of food for other travelers.

For example, in 1882, an Italian boat "Vettor Pesani" and its crew decided to pay a visit to the interior of the island. To their great surprise, they found the island brimming with potential. The green fields were filled with cattle and the trees heavy with fruit. The ranch house was empty but still usable. They did not see a soul and so they filled their hold with fresh foods and left wondering what had happened.

In 1887, the French corvette, "Decres", under the command of G. Estienne passed by the island and has left us a description of Valdizán's house.

"Sunday May 15, I set sail for Floriana Island. This island is interesting to visit because a portion of its territory was bought some time ago by the Frenchman, M. Leon Iturburu and on information that I received in Guayaquil, I assumed the island was being worked. That is not the case at all. Upon walking around the island, following the map, we found no signs of houses or any population. The animals had reverted to their wild state. There are no inhabitants and of the house on the beach, the only thing left are the roof framework and beams. On the road that leads inland, at an elevation of some 200 meters, one can see at a distance the house that was undoubtably used by Valdizan in his last years on the island. This house is a large hut with remains of iron rods and sides that are made of a double layer of bamboo. The floor is off the ground and is still in good condition. There is a beautiful vineyard on the east side of the house. Of the terrace outside the house, the posts and banisters still remain. The grave site of the owner is located some 50 feet from the house. A black cross dominates the tomb, with a small fence surrounding it. There is a small sign with the following inscription: "Here lie the venerable remains of Mr. Jose Valdizan, G. (8) P. D., died July 23, 1878.

" Close to this tomb is another with a cross with only these words; "B. Pozo".

CHAPTER VI.

THE SMALL EMPIRE OF
MANUEL J. COBOS IN GALAPAGOS
1879 – 1904

On February 17, 1904, Guayaquil was greatly excited by the news that a sloop with eighty fugitives from the Galapagos Islands had been captured in Tumaco, on the southwestern coast of Colombia. They had fled there after committing at least two murders and perhaps many more. Anything could be expected from the inhabitants of those islands given their bad reputation at that time.

Three days later, the presumed criminals arrived and were seen by the thousands of people who crowded into the port. Seventy—eight men, eight women and four children disembarked in the custody of two columns of police. While some of them certainly had a sinister air, the majority were ordinary peasants from the Ecuadorian coast, poorly dressed and seemingly harmless.

They were taken to the municipal jail to await the trial that would be held to judge the principals and accomplices in the murders. The court began its sessions, but at the same time the press published not only the declarations of the prisoners, but also the protests of many people who questioned the reasons for establishing a concentration camp in the Galapagos for the benefit of only one person, with the apparent backing of the authorities.

The murderer and ringleader was a Colombian mulatto named Elias Puertas, who didn't deny the deed. Quite the contrary, he affirmed that it was the only way to liberate the slaves on Chatham Island. The other prisoners, the majority of whom had not taken part in the murders, proclaimed him "The Liberator" and corroborated Puertas' declarations.

There had been two murders, that of the plantation's owner,

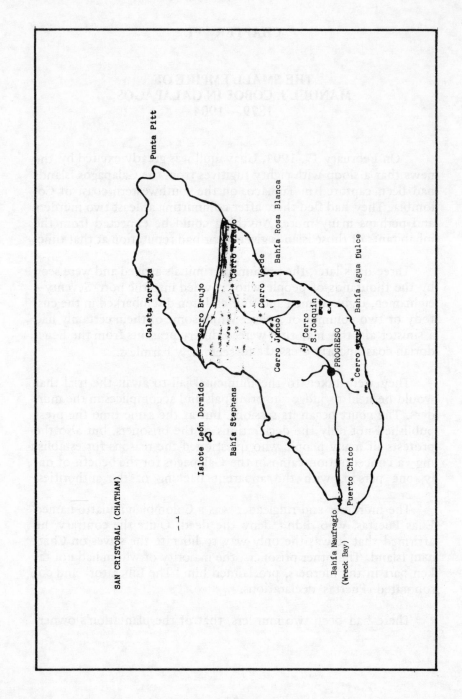

Don Manuel J. Cobos and that of the Territorial Head, Don Leonardo Reyna. The people had sacked the rooms and burned the record papers, but that was all. Many of them seemed to be innocent victims of a system of exploitation that had lasted too long.

A commission was sent to the Galapagos to install the new officials, receive the declarations of the witnesses, carry out autopsies of the victims and gather all possible information about life on the island.

The arrival of the Commission on San Cristobal Island caused panic among the inhabitants, because it was only then that they learned of the capture of the first group of fugitives. But, above all, the people assumed that they would be accused and the law would go against them, as had always happened in the past. They would not have anyone to turn to. The population was very poor and, contrary to the information that had been received, fewer than the majority were criminals.

The Commission saw many new things: a very productive plantation and a modern mill which were the center of many activities. The plantation was the site of incredible progress in spite of the difficult conditions on the island. Unfortunately , a negative social reality was also evident: a system of forced work and slavery for a miserable salary in leather, copper or paper money. These could only be cashed at the employer's store, paying the prices he imposed. Many workers had been laboring on the plantation for years with no hope of returning to the mainland. Without legal controls on the island, Cobos the employer, determined salaries and fines, lengthened or ended contracts. The scars on the backs of the workers spoke of frequent whippings for failing to carry out a task, for losing a sheep attacked by savage dogs or for rebellion.

The new authorities were sworn into office and, together with the Commission, gathered information about the recent events. The complaints against the owner of the plantation were numerous. Some of them seemed exaggerated, such as exile to uninhabited islands, the rape of women and even adolescent girls by Cobos, shootings and whippings that had caused the death of various people. The questions that everyone asked were: What was the role of the authorities in all this drama? Why had Leonardo Reyna, the Territorial Head been murdered? Had the authorities been incompetent or were they accomplices to these arbitrary acts? The autopsies were carried out, confirming the cause of death, as well as revealing other details, such as Cobos's syphilis.

The population was living in unhealthy conditions. Mixing criminal elements with an already difficult population had created serious problems. There was a great disproportion between men and women and tensions ran high. Several men frequently shared a woman.

One day the Commission heard the case of a prostitute who had stabbed a man, trying to kill him because of her jealousy. All the information that was brought to the attention to the Commission indicated that the Island was neither a paradise nor exclusively the lair of criminals.

Another Commission returned to the Galapagos two months later to clear up several questions, including the rescue of Camilo Casanova who had been exiled by Cobos to Indefatigable Island (Santa Cruz), which was uninhabited at that time.

Several questions were asked at that time and they have been repeated even since. Among them were: What was the real world of Manuel J. Cobos?. How could that concentration camp have existed for so many years if the authorities were not accomplices?

We will try to answer these two questions.

Who was Don Manuel J. Cobos?

Manuel J. Cobos was born in Cuenca in 1836. He worked in commerce from a very early age, first with his brother Angel, and later with José Monroy, who was from Guayaquil. For unknown reasons Cobos and Monroy set up their base of operations in the village of Chanduy, west of Guayaquil. They traded intensively all along the Ecuadorian coast. In 1866, they extended their commercial activities to the Galapagos, where they pretended to be exploiting the wild cattle for the leather business. They acquired some land on Chatham Island (San Cristobal) and set up their base of operations there. The new merchants with their fleet of sloops were able to take advantage of the isolations of the Archipelago for their favorite activity, contraband. And so it was that the Cobos—Monroy ships left Chatham for Panama. They sold leather and products from the island there, filled their ships with foreign products and ended the voyage in Chanduy, as if they were coming from the Galapagos.

MANUEL J. COBOS

Owner of the Hacienda El Progreso on San Cristobal Island. He was murdered January 15, 1904. In formal dress (above) and work clothes (below).

During the following years, they had to face various trials for contraband and for killing cattle belonging to other people, as well as for their attempt to take over Charles Island, which belonged legally to the Villamil family. Cobos evaded the trials by hiding on Chatham, where he enlarged his properties, while his partner Monroy faced the judges in Guayaquil.

During the same period, archil, a lichen highly appreciated by dyers, was discovered on the islands and Cobos began exploiting it to the fullest. Unfortunately for him, Don Gabriel García Moreno became President of Ecuador and auctioned off the exclusive rights to the exploitation of archil in 1869. Don José Valdizan of Charles Island received these rights. Cobos didn't dare compete with him because the President had signed a warrant for his arrest. It was an annoying frustration, but it wasn't hard to evade. In Mexico (Baja California), large fields of archil had just been discovered and Cobos saw a great opportunity there because of the experience he had acquired. The two inseparable partners, Cobos and Monroy, traveled to Mexico with a contract from a North American firm. Meanwhile the fields of Chatham remained under the care of twelve families who were responsible for maintaining the crops and felling the forest to make pastures.

The following year found José Monroy recruiting workers in Guayaquil and once more again having problems with the Governor of Guayas Province. He intended to recruit army deserters and men who had problems with the law and take them to Mexico. Monroy made at least three voyages in his small sloops, taking 70 workers each time. They followed the route Guayaquil—Galápagos México, stopping for supplies at Cobos and Monroy properties on the islands.

At first, the custom of recruiting men who had problems with the law and who could turn against him may seem strange. But judging by his later behavior, this was to his great advantage because he could treat them and pay them as he pleased and they did not dare file any complaints with the authorities.

The price of archil fell in the decade of the 1870's when. European chemists developed dyes which were much cheaper. Cobos and Monroy returned and installed themselves on Chatham with a few loyal workers. Their definite plans included taking over all of the arable land on the island and, if it were possible, in the entire Archipelago. They also planned to exploit the wild cattle for the leather and salted meat business, kill turtles for their oil, and catch fish.

Cobos's luck was at its zenith: García Moreno had been assassinated a few years earlier, as had his competitor Don Jose Valdizan on Charles Island. The latter's workers didn't want to remain on an island that seemed doomed and they agreed to go to work for Cobos. Almost a hundred of them moved to Chatham in 1879.

The center and starting point for the small empire was the plantation, El Progreso, about 8 kilometers from Puerto Chico known today as Baquerizo Moreno, where Cobos personally directed the work. José Monroy, was established in Guayaquil as representative, correspondent, coordinator and provisioner for the El Progreso plantation.

Manuel J. Cobos was 42 years old, but he appeared much younger. He had untiring energy, extraordinary initiative and creativity, but above all, he had an incredible commercial vision. Unfortunately it was an unscrupulous commercial sense. Cobos was single. He had never been married, but at that time he had two children, Manuel Adolfo and Josefina.

To begin developing his grandiose plans, he had at his disposition about 120 men, an entire island, no one who would compete with him and no authority who could limit his ambition.

The splendor of the Empire.

The fields of Chatham were filled with pastures and plantations of all types, especially sugar cane for the manufacture of syrup and liquor. At the same time, Cobos sent his teams of hunters after the cattle that wandered about the island. In 1890, the

Territorial Head calculated that there were still about 10,000 head of cattle. This was doubtless an exaggeration, but, in any case, they must have still been very abundant. The hides were made into leather and some of the meat was sold as jerky, that is salted and dried.

Another item of intense exploitation was turtle oil. Cobos' teams of "oilers" quickly exterminated the species of tortoises native to southern Chatham. They then turned to the tortoise population on Charles, which met the same fate: finally, they went on to the tortoises of Albemarle. No one will ever know how many tortoises were slaughtered but it is sure to have been several thousand.

Chatham Island was transformed into a productive plantation that nourished a population of 200 inhabitants and maintained an active trade with Guayaquil. Two vessels sailed back and forth between the island and the Mainland where José Monroy was in charge of selling the products.

The Sugar Mill.

After a few years machinery for the manufacture of sugar arrived and the majority of the cultivated area was transformed into sugar cane fields. The 50 initial blocks planted in cane rose to 150 in 1887 and, finally, to 400 in 1904.

(Stein Hoff: Drommem om Galapagos, 1985, p. 106 San Cristobal : The sugar mill of El Progreso in 1926.

Modern machinery was installed in 1889 and from that moment the plantation became an industrial center with the infrastructure necessary to serve the sugar mill. Pure water was brought down to the plant from the mountains over a distance of eight kilometers by canals and aqueducts. A small "Decauville style railroad" with portable rails and hauled by oxen, was imported to facilitate transportation of the sugar cane. In the last years of the empire, they were preparing to import a steam locomotive to accelerate transportation. A network of roads had been built which left the port and reached all points of the plantation. A wooden dock facilitated the loading and unloading of the boats and near it there were great warehouses to store the products for export.

RUINS OF OVENS and ROADS OF EL PROGRESO SUGAR MILL A railroad drawn by oxen ran over the roads.

The sugar production continued to grow until it reached 20,000 hundredweight a year, besides native rum and panela (raw brown sugar). Not satisfied with that, Cobos experimented with new products, especially coffee, which came to cover several hectares with more than 100,000 trees. Before his death, he had introduced the cultivation of agave, grapes and other plants. Cacao was the only plant whose cultivation was not successful, but that was a small failure in the midst of so much success.

The population of the empire.

An industrial, agricultural, ranching, fishing and commercial complex, such as the one described, could not sustain itself without a large work force and a carefully structured economic system. These were soon attained. The number of workers grew with the needs of the plantation and the sugar mill. In 1887, there were 200 ; this number grew to 300 when the factory was installed and passed 400 in 1904.

We have already seen how the first groups arrived. Later growth was due to a very clever move by Cobos and Monroy. Many volunteers, dazzled by the promises made to them, arrived and after them, their relatives; then came some foreigners (Colombians and Peruvians) who were unable to find work in the Mainland.

The island's fame as a conglomerate of criminals was the result of the deportation of some criminals in order to empty the jails. But, above all, it was the result of an arrangment between the authorities and Cobos to send pickpockets, petty thieves, confirmed vagrants and anyone the police considered a nuisance, to Chatham. When Cobos' boats arrived in Guayaquil, these prisoners were secretly embarked for the islands, where supposedly they would be converted into good citizens.

A more numerous group was made up of imprisoned debtors. Cobos paid the creditor through Monroy and later that sum was recovered many times over. The debtors were forced to pay for their passage, their mantenance, risks and interest. The salary they earned was so small (50 sucres a year) that it was impossible to save a cent. Also, their sentences could be extended indefinitely. A fine, even it is only a few sucres, became another link in the chain that bound these workers to Cobos's plantation.

Jeronimo Beltran, the most bloodthirsty of the murderers, arrived to the Galapagos with his mother, when he was a child of ten, following his father who had believed in Cobos' promises. After his mother and later his father died, Jeronimo, who was fourteen at the time, had to accept a debt of 140 sucres. By 1904, it had grown to 754 sucres. He was enslaved for life.

The case of Jerónimo who began to work very young was not rare. Many of the fugitives captured in Tumaco were between 25 and 30 years old and they had been working in the islands for more than 10 years. It was undoubtedly a very practical method of achieving submission. The women, many of whom had bad reputations, had arrived in the same way.

This system of recruiting workers with problems was convenient, although it had its risks. Since the prison and police authorities of Guayaquil had become accomplices of the system, they were unable to protest about the arbitrariness or the injustice, no mater what treatment the workers were given.

The arrival of a new group of workers at the plantation seemed festive because the ordinary labor was suspended to unload the boats, lodge the new arrivals, and even organize a dance in the evening. But the following day, everyone, whether volunteers or prisoners, without distinction, had to accept the same discipline, methods, salaries and rates of the plantation. Those who accepted unconditionally, were treated less harshly or even kindly, but the independent ones or those who demanded their rights, could expect the worst, yet another means of exacting submission.

The population was made up largely of men with a disproportionately small number of women. In the best of times, there were four men for one women , but at other times the ratio was eight to one. The consequences of this abnormal situation could be foreseen. Polyandry was frequent and reactions during the sadly renowned dances, when alcohol lowered the inhibitions of the inhabitants, often ended in violence or even deaths.

The English voyager Alex Mann, who visited the plantation, expressed the problem this way:

> Two causes, I am convinced, have occasioned the insurrections and crimes perpetrated on these

islands: the first, perhaps not the principal, the intermixture of criminals with respectable laborers; the second, the overlooking of one of nature's primary laws, a due proportion between the sexes . . . with the concomitant vices of gambling and mad infatuation for liquor or other stimulants, when desperation transforms many a law—abiding man into a reckless villain".

The system of life and work.

The day's work began very early at 4 a. m. in order to take advantage of the daylight and it lasted up to 14 hours or even more when it was necessary to load or unload a boat, or during the "zafra", or sugar cane harvest. A communal meal was served at noon; it was the unappetizing "pingui", a stew of meat, fish and unpeeled plantains, generally those left over in the store. Only an undernourished worker's hunger could make him eat such an awful tasting dish.

FELIPE LASTRE

A Mexican, one of Cobos's most loyal workers. He came with him from México in 1879. He directed the work of bringing water from the mountains to El Progreso.

PRIVATE MONEY FROM EL PROGRESO

Made of rubber, copper and paper. It could be used only to buy goods in the hacienda's stores.

They worked seven days a week and there were only three holidays in the year. January 1st, Mardi Gras and the owner's birthday. On the latter day, work ended early at 2 p.m. and at sunset a dance was held in a dark and foul—smelling building. On other occasions, when new workers arrived from Guayaquil, when Cobos wanted to present a homage to one of his right hand men, or when they needed to empty some tanks of cane rum, the day's work ended at 4 p.m.

Wages, at it was said, were extremely low and paid in leather or copper coins or in IOU's which could only be cashed in the plantation store. With such an income it was impossible to save anything and, in any case, this money obviously wasn't accepted on the continent.

After 25 years on the island, Felipe Lastra, one of the most loyal workers who had come with Cobos from Mexico, had no possessions and felt a sense of panic as he looked forward to a destitute old age.

The authorities.

In 1885 the Ecuadorian Congress abolished the "Galapagos Province" and transformed it into an "Island Territory", with a Territorial Chief, a notary and an inspector with six policemen at his command. Unfortunately, the conditions under which those authorities had to work could not have been more absurd. The population of Chatham, the only inhabited island at that time, consisted of the Cobo's workers. Therefore, the authorities were, in practice, collaborators of the plantation owner. Besides, from the moment they set foot on the island, they depended on him for food, water, transportation and sometimes even for housing. Under these circumstances, opposing the island's owner meant a certain death or, at least resignation.

There was a case of a Territorial Chief, colonel Irigoyen (1893) who dared stand up to Cobos and criticize his methods and unjust punishments, but he did it when an Ecuadorian Navy vessel was anchored in the port. Cobos had imposed the punishment of 500 lashes on a woman, María Agustina Farias. This could possibly lead to her death. The ex—Territorial Chief brought the plantation owner to trial, but nothing came of it for lack of witnesses. This situation explains why this empire of injustice lasted for a quarter of a century (1879—1904).

The punishments

Such a system could not sustain itself without an efficient method of control, spying, and punishment. There was a very efficient chain of informers made up of men Cobos considered trustworthy; opportunists who were ready to denounce anyone for a privilege or a small gift; prostitutes, and sometimes, even children.

Punishments and reprisals for small faults and rebellious attitudes went from whippings up to exile on deserted islands or even death from a firing squad. The sentences of whipping reached such horryfying levels (500 or 600 lashes) that they sometimes caused death. Those who remained in poor condition afterwards were locked in an isolated room called the jail, where they were found a few days later, dead and eaten by the rats.

Unfulfilled tasks of hunters or fishermen were punished with 50 lashes for a tanned skin not turned in or for an incomplete catch of fish. During the 1904 trial, a journalist commented, "As if the wild cattle and the fish were there waiting for the hunters or fishers"! . .How many died as a result of the public whippings? At least ten were named during the trial.

The most dreaded punishment was exile to a desert island; it was equivalent of a death penalty if one were unable to find water. The declarations of 1904 gave the names of at least 15 men who were exiled, many of whom were never heard from again. Two skeletons were found by foreign ships on James Island (Santiago). Adolf Beck gave the following description of one of these discoveries. "There was the skeleton of a man with a few things scattered around him, under a piece of canvas held up by some logs to protect him from the suffocating sun. It is certain that this was the body of Raymundo Cuadrado, another of the victims that Cobos had exiled and condemned to a terrible death".

Some survived, mainly on Indefatigable Island (Santa Cruz). A man named Murillo was located by a scientific expedition and mercifully taken to Albemarle Island. The best—known case is that of Camilo Casanova who survived and was rescued by the second commission sent after Cobos death.

The most notable deaths before a firing squad occurred in 1886 when a conspiracy was discovered. Six men were arrested. Since the goverment authorities had not yet arrived, Cobos wanted to give a warning, but he cynically tried to put on the appearance of a democracy. He organized a plebiscite! Everyone had to vote publicly. The conspirators were condemned without a single vote in their favor. Everyone knew that such a vote would only increase the number of the victims. They were shot by a firing squad. The life of Manuel Olaya, one of the workers who had arrived in 1879, was saved by the intercession of the administrator of the plantation, an Argentinian, and by his own wife. The memory of those shootings was engraved in everyone's mind and it was reborn on the day of the murders, as we shall soon see.

The Conspiracy. January 1904.

After twenty—five years, the Cobos's Empire was at its peak; it continued growing and everything it undertook bore fruit. Manuel J. Cobos was 67 years old but his vigor was undiminished. His methods of achieving submission and repression kept the population apparently calm. He could think about new projects. It was rumored, however, that he was planning to sell everything to a North American company and retire to Lima, where he planned to marry a lady whose last name was Tabara. It was said that the price offered for the plantation was 500,000 dollars, an enormous sum for that time.

Cobos had never married, although he had two children: Manuel Adolfo and Josefina. Manuel Adolfo was a young man very similar to his father who had begun to work on the plantation at the end of the century. He had died shortly thereafter as the result of a fall onto a sharply pointed stick while hunting on horseback. The wound became infected and he was sent to Cuenca, where he died soon afterwards. Josefina lived in Guayaquil and after the death of her brother, she was apple of her father's eye.

The workers' desire to free themselves was not achieved after the events of 1886, but, in spite of everything, it remained latent. The conspiracy of 1904 was successful because of the presence of a very capable leader, the Colombian, ELIAS PUERTAS.

The conspiracy began with the loss (or theft) of a revolver, which mysteriously came into the hands of Puertas. If the conspirators wanted to eliminate the owner, this was a unique opportunity. This occurred at the end of 1903.

Later tales tell of the alternatives considered by the conspirators. The first was sending a communication to Guayaquil in an attempt to expose the true situation of the population. When that was difficult to carry out, they proposed that the cook, José Jaime, eliminate Cobos. The last alternative was that of setting fire to the sugar cane fields. This could give them a chance to kill Cobos under cover of the confusion and the running around of the people.

The first solution is hypothetical, if it was really considered, because, although it would indicate that the conspirators were not so perverse as was supposed, it was impossible. It would be a case of the Ecuadorian proverb: "Dovers against guns", the Galapagos workers, known as criminals, would be pitted against Cobos and authorities in the courts of Guayaquil. It didn't make sense. The second possibility, that of the cook, was discarded when the conspirators saw the fear and terror that José Jaime felt when they placed the weapon in his hands. Only the last possibility remained: a fire in the sugar cane fields.

The number of the conspirators must have been either very large or badly selected, because the news soon filtered down to the spies. Through them it reached Cobos, who reacted decisively, although he didn't seem to take the threat seriously, as we shall see later.

ELIAS PUERTAS
Leader of the conspiracy which ended the life of Manuel J. Cobos on January 15th; 1904.

HOUSE OF MANUEL j. COBOS ON SAN CRISTOBAL

Cobos threw himself from the window marked "1" after being gravely wounded on January 15th, 1904.

Don Manuel attempted to identify the heads of the conspiracy by punishing certain persons whom he suspected. On the 12th of January, two workers, Parra and Garcia, were sentenced to receive 300 lashes. The following day it was the turn of Juan Ignacio Torres. Cobos obtained nothing, but the tension of the conspirators increased and there was always someone who spoke imprudently. Jose Prieto, a black Colombian who was protected by Puertas was heard to say, "When will the day come when we will see the fields on fire?". In an atmosphere of expectation, this phrase would be a revealing clue. He was taken prisoner that same day, and placed on the bar to receive 400 lashes the following day. When he heard that decision, the Territorial Head, Leonardo Reyna exclaimed: "It must be 500, because I have an order from the Governor of Guayaquil to beat them and even to send them before the firing squad '. If he really said that, then he had signed his dead sentence.

José Prieto was far from being an angel. A vagrant, a heavy drinker and quarrelsome, he had the reputation of being incorrigible and he had already suffered Cobos' "justice" several times. The news of Prieto's imprisonment fell like lightening on the conspirators and they turned to Elias Puertas. They knew Prieto and they were sure he would talk and if he did, that would be the end of all of them. The only solution was to get ahead of Cobos and eliminate him. The only one who could do that was Puertas. The important thing that night was to keep the other conspirators quiet and assure them that the "coup" would not fail, in order to avoid last minute betrayals.

No one slept that night. The conspirators counted the hours until dawn; Puertas kept turning the details on the plan over his head. The plantation bell struck the hour and another repeated from the sugar mill. It was the only clock and the shifts were maintained regularly during the night.

Manuel J. Cobos couldn't sleep that night either because of a syphilitic ulcer on his leg that had put him in a bad mood during the day.

The 15th of January dawned.

Elias Puertas, like all of the superintendents, got up at four in order to organize the work. At that time there was already movement in the town. The shifts at the sugar mill and the guards in the owner's house changed at three in the morning. Manuel Morán, the policeman on duty, sat down sleepily in the living room next to Cobos's room, leaned his gun in a corner and began to doze.

Elias Puertas threw on a poncho to protect himself from the morning chill and headed down the road, holding the revolver with two bullets tightly in his hand. On the road, he passed by the engineer, Mr. Campbell, who was in charge of the sugar mill. They greeted one another and continued on to their destinations as they did every day. It was beginning to get light and the finches sang their songs from the fences. It was almost five o' clock in the morning. Various workers were headed towards the owner's house to seek permissions or favors. On the ground floor of the plantation house, Daniel Zabala, Cobos's godson, opened the store where they handed out a little shot of liquor as they called the roll and gave out job orders.

José Jaime, the cook, went uptairs to prepare breakfast for the owner and several of his friends took advantage of a few minutes for a cup of coffee, ran behind him.

Near the entrance of the house Puertas met Pancho Valverde, an old man loyal to Cobos. "Old Man— he said hugging him— "intercede with the master to free Prieto from the whipping he has been sentenced to receive". Valverde answered him saying that it was impossible because his master was determined to discover everything and set an example, and his decision was irrevocable. Then he added: 'Today there's going to be a great dispute on this plantation: I would rather die than see it".

Then Puertas asked if the master was sleeping, and Valverde answered affirmatively. Puertas said, "I want to ask for some permissions for some of the workers and I also need to receive today's orders".

While this dialogue was going on, several conspirators mixed with the workers who were coming up to the house and placed themselves at strategic points. One of the them, Uldarico García, stopped calling the roll and ran uptairs to wake the owner. Cobos came out a few minutes later in his underwear and in a very bad mood because of the sleepless night he had spent. He sat down in a rocking chair just outside of his bedroom and called Carlitos Romero who tended to his wound. Several workers came up to ask for permission not to work that day, but all requests were abruptly denied while he observed the boy's work.

Puertas was standing up in the back, nervously holding the revolver and following all of the owner's movements with his eyes. Cobos looked up, expecting another petition. The superintendent moved a few steps forward while asking for permission for some other workers. It was sharply denied. After waiting for a few seconds, he decided to ask for a pardon for his fellow countryman, Prieto. The refusal was an even sharper "NO!"

Some author has added a longer answer: "You know that my orders here are carried out in every detail and Prieto's public whiping will be executed today at seven, in my presence. Whoever is guilty in the project to set fire to the sugar cane fields will be immediately sent before the firing squad".

The dice were thrown!

The testimony of those who were present, the policeman Moran and the boy, Carlos Romero, coincides as to what happened immediately afterwards.

"Don Manuel, You are not going to beat Prieto?."

"Yes".

"You are not going to kill any more!"

THE SCENE OF THE CRIME
The rocking chair where Cobos sat and where he was wounded. At the rear is the door to his bedroom. The treasury (first door) Where he kept the hacienda's accounts and the weapons of the State.

In his declarations, Puertas added, ' His tyrannical conduct cut his life short . . . and taking out his revolver I shot him twice", once through the chest and once in the stomach, diagonally from the left. Cobos got up and staggered towards his room. The first one to react was the conspirator, Pedro Jiménez , who ran up from behind and gave Cobos two superficial cuts in the head with his machete.

RUINS OF COBOS'S HOUSE

In the foreground are the steps which went up to the second floor where Elías Ramírez was wounded.

Things had happened so rapidly that everyone was paralyzed for a few moments: Puertas, Romero, Morán the policeman . . . . . As the door closed behind the wounded man, Moran grabbed for his gun, but other conspirators were faster and they stopped him. Carlitos Romero fled to the kitchen and ran into José Jaime who was coming out after having heard the shots. Puertas came in too and demanded that the cook take part in the action. They heard shouts of joy from downstairs and then a mob was coming up the stairs. Suddenly a shot sounded. Elias Ramirez was bleeding from his arm. From his room, Cobos attempted to fire again, but the firearm jammed. Every one was trying to hide in the side rooms and some people forced open the doors to the accounting office where the government weapons were stored. Some shots were heard, and all left the house armed with pistols and guns.

Cobos didn't reappear. The first bullet had perforated his left lung, causing a massive hemorrage; the second had passed through his intestine, also causing serious injury. Cobos was mortally wounded.

Puertas freed Prieto and Carranza and left the house where he found other mutineers, who didn't know what to do next. He shouted, "Follow me", and headed for the house of the Territorial Head which was located a slight distance away. This official had been advised of the events and the policeman Fuentes has insisted that he should flee. Leonardo Reyna refused because he thought that the workers had nothing against him and in any case, he had a pistol and two policemen with him. When he saw the mob coming, he got dressed and waited for them at the window, while the two policemen disappeared behind the house. The following moments were filled with confusion and given the fact that is was still dark (5:15 a.m.), it wasn't possible for those who were present to reconstruct what happened. Leonardo Reyna jumped out of the window and begged, "I give up, don't kill me, I'm a poor old man and the head of a family". There was a moment of doubt and nobody moved, but someone (there are those who said that it was Puertas), shouted, "Kill the old bandit", and then, "Make way".

A shot was heard and Reyna fell dead. The bullet shot at close range entered through his neck and destroyed the organs in the thoracic cavity. A few moments of silence followed. Jerónimo Beltrán pushed his way through, came up to the postrate man and stabbed him in the stomach with an enormous knife.

Seeing that he was dead, they returned to Cobos' house. They didn't know if Cobos was dead or alive, but the reigning silence was a favorable sign for the rebels. So they rushed forward, craving the blood of the hated owner. They tried to break down the door, but the locks did not yield easily.

Cobos, realizing that the situation was hopeless, leaped from the bedroom window, hoping to escape through the stable. The height was great for anyone and more so for a seriously injured man. When he fell, he broke a leg and moments later he died.

One of workers had been able to discern Cobos' intentions in the semi—darkness and he gave a warning at the same time as those upstairs broke down the door. They entered the bedroom, went to the window, and fired several shots at the inert body below. The shooting didn't last long because the mob ran to the stable to dispach Cobos, who was in final agony. Everyone fell on him, hitting him, kicking him, beating him with rifle butts, etc. Once again the last act of horror was performed by Jerónimo, who thrust his knife into Cobos' abdomen.

At the conclusion of this terrible drama, the mob set about sacking the bedroom and the accounting office. Money, clothing and objects of value disappeared. The account books where the debts and accounts of the workers were registered, were taken out of the office. A bonfire was lit which reduced all of the plantation's accounting to ashes. Elias Puertas at the request of all, opened the store and distributed supplies to eveyone present.

DON LEONARDO REYNA

Territorial Head of Galapagos. He was murdered - together with Cobos on January 15, 1904.

At that moment the danger was the passion that had been un-
leashed against the authorities, collaborators and spies of Cobos.
The most exalted of the men wanted to kill them all, but Puertas
imposed order and avoided any more bloodshed. Those who were
threatened at that moment were the police, Mr. Campbell, the engineer and the Deputy, who lived in the port.

When everyone had calmed down, Campbell intervened with
Puertas to mediate with the Deputy and ask him for the firearms
in order to avoid any further bloodshed. And that is what was
done. It was difficult to control the passion of certain individuals,
so Puertas had to take drastic measures; he had to get rid of all of
the liquor at the sugar mill. He opened the faucets of the vats
until the last drop had been spilled.

Again Campbell intervened to hold a wake and bury the dead
in a dignified manner. Puertas's intention had been to cremate
them, but in a demonstration of self—respect he gave the permission. They brought Cobos' corpse up to the main living room
and that of Leonardo Reyna to the government house. Meanwhile,
Federico Salazar built the coffins as quickly as possible. Curiously,
Federico Salazar had also built the coffin for José Valdizán on
Charles Island 26 years before.

A few loyal workers accompanied the bodies during the hours
that they waited before burying them. Among them were Francisco Valverde who had accompanied Cobos to México, Federico
Lastre, the Mexican and his son Santiago.

When the crude coffins were finished, the bodies were placed
in them, covered only by a sheet, and the funeral was held immediately. Even so, the desire for revenge had not yet been satisfied.
At the suggestion of Heliodoro Quiñóñez, one of angriest men, it
was decided that they should be buried in the same place where
the five workers had been sent before the firing squad in 1886.

A few loyal friends carried the coffins and at five o'clock in
the afternoon they were lowered into the graves and covered with
a thin layer of earth without any special ceremony. Thus, in the

midst of a lugubrious silence, that tragic day ended.

The conspirators' concern during the following days was to leave the island as soon as possible in one of the plantation's sloops. One of these was out fishing and the other should arrive in a few days from Guayaquil. The first, "Josephine Cobos", was taken with deceit and 78 men, 8 women and 4 children embarked, after loading 200 hundredweight of sugar to sell to raise money on the mainland.

Emilio Haensen, a German was forced to pilot the ship because he understood a little about navigation. He did it well, even though he did not have navigation instruments. The fugitives' plan was to head for Mexico or Central America, but Haensen took them to Tumaco, in southern Colombia. The first days were no problem, although they didn't have their navigating papers. The problem came when the fugitives accused Haensen of selling the sugar for his own benefit. The German denounced them to the Colombian authorities and so the short period of liberty ended.

TOMB OF MANUEL J. COBOS
Today empty, on the spot where five workers were shot in 1886.

Epilogue.

The trial that took place in Guayaquil was long and difficult, because apart from the problem of distance, there were the irregularities of the authorities, and the system of oppression of the island to be considered. A number of lawyers began to ask if, given the conditions under which the workers of Chatham had lived, they were justified in taking the law in their own hands.

Elias Puertas tried to put all of the blame on himself, which won him the respect of his companions and a great part of the city. The majority of the others were freed within a few days, although the situation of those poor people was desperate. They had nothing and many of them had never even seen money. The city took up a collection and helped in many ways. Some cases were pathetic, such as that of the family of Manuel Olaya, who had not participated in the murders, but who had suffered a great deal under Cobos. He had returned after being in Chatham for 25 ye·

Elías Puertas and one other man were condemned to several years of prison. The others were freed. Although they had participated in the mutiny, their guilt had been erased considering the suffering of the earlier years.

The Judgement of History.

It is difficult to evaluate the personality and the works of Manuel J. Cobos because there are both good and bad aspects. To some extent when trying to make a judgement the hierarchy of values by which ones lives weighs heavily. Instead of prolonged examination about the merits of Cobos, we are going to transcribe here the judgements of two men who were very close to the happenings and one of them had dealt with Cobos personally, Nicolas Martínez and Alex Mann. The first was a writer from Ambato who spent a season in the Galapagos two years after the murder of Cobos and the second was an English traveler who had spent long periods of time in Guayaquil and the Archipelago.

Martínez wrote as follows:

"Upon seeing the machinery and observing the flourishing state of the plantation, one could not but admire the energy and constancy which Cobos must have developed in order to obtain these results . . . Don Manuel J. Cobos may be as bad as they assure us and even a criminal as they say, but even so we can not help but recognize in him a man of prodigious energy and indomitable character; only an individual who possessed these talents could have formed a plantation of the magnitude of "El Progreso' an a deserted island, without sufficient capital, without communications with inhabited places, and have attained this using exclusively the waste of society. . .

I think that is very difficult to judge Cobos because it is necessary to put oneself in his place, taking in consideration the class of men who surrounded him . . . I, after having heard both sides, don't consider myself capable of judging Cobos and for that reason, I do nothing more than recognize in him his great character and his indomitable energy, without daring to condemn or justify his actions . . ." (1)

On the other hand Alex Mann had this to say:

"The warf, roads, water—supply and cultivated fields, in a place where, before his time, desolation reigned supreme, are monuments to his indomitable energy; but when one reflects on his inhumanity our homage is clouded by abhorrence of the infamous means he employed. I was acquainted with Manuel Cobos, and found him a most pleasant conversationalist, fairly educated, practical and even humorous, and honorable in his business engagements, reminding me

(1)   Martínez, Nicolas: "Impresiones de un viaje", Quito, 1911, pp. 96-97.

of Byron's pirate, 'the mildest mannered man that ever scuttled ship or cut a throat".

He lived for twenty—five years, an autocrat among a criminal community, carrying his life at his revolver belt, and ruling with a rod of iron. He had redeeming points in his character, but in that settlement the field for humanity was circumscribed; in a civilized country, retrained by efficient laws, Manuel Cobos would have been an able pioneer of progress and respected citizen". (1)

It is hard to add anything more except to say that the "monuments to his indomitable energy" have been ephemeral and only ruins remain. On the other hand, the extinction of the tortoises on Chatham and Charles Island, the destruction and the reversals of the ecology on his island have been permanent.

We will let the reader decide, according to his criteria, which is more important, economic results or human values.

(1) Alex Mann. "Yatching in the Pacific", London 1909. pp. 35-36.

Further Readings.

Anonimous, "Los Crímenes de Galápagos.— El Pirata del Guayas, Asesinato de Valdizán, Asesinato de Cobos y Reyna", Guayaquil, 1904.

Bognoly-Espinoza: "Las Islas Encantadas o el Archipiélago de Colón", Guayaquil, 1905.

Latorre, Octavio: El pequeño Imperio de Manuel J. Cobos en Galápagos", Guayaquil, 1991.

Martínez, N. Impresiones de un viaje, Quito, 1911, 1917.

BROAD FIELDS UNDER CULTIVATION OF THE HACIENDA EL PROGRESO.
Today these are almost entirely abandoned

CHAPTER VII

THREE YEARS IN SOLITARY ON SANTA CRUZ ISLAND

The Case of Camilo Casanova 1900 - 1904

One of the punishments meted out by Manuel Cobos to discipline his rebellious workers was banishment to a deserted island, from which some never returned. Ultimately, it was this kind of cruel behaviour that was Cobos' undoing and during the trial for the assassination the following names of his former workers stand out· Jose Hurtado, Otilio Carrion, Heliodoro Quiñones, Fidel Mora, Jose Cortez, Daniel Fajardo, Raymundo Guardado, Camilo Casanova and some 15 more.

The fate of the unlucky exiles depended totally on the availability of water and as we know, of the uninhabited islands only Santa Cruz has water year round and Santiago only at certain times of the year. And so anyone abandoned on Santiago would die of thirst. This was the fate of Fajardo and Raymundo Guardado whose bodies were found by a scientific expedition of 1905. The remains of Guardado left a clear picture of what his last days night have been like; hoping for a rescue, his remains lay scattered about next to some utensils under the remains of an old tent which must have protected him from the sun.

The workers sent to Chavez or Santa Cruz Island could take advantage of the fresh water springs and even cultivate some of the more fertile grounds. At the end of the century a Mr. N. Murillo was abandoned there. Nothing was known about him for a long time until the account of another scientific expedition that spoke of his rescue and transfer to Isabella Island.

Chavez island or Indefatigable (Santa Cruz) is located at a relatively short distance from San Cristobal and on a clear day it's possible to see it on the horizon. It is one of the most beautiful islands but for some reason it never attracted colonizers until late this century. Manuel Cobos frequently used Santa Cruz as a place of banishment for unruly workers, the last of whom was Camilo Casanova.

Camilo, born in Rio Chico in the province of Manabí, was a soldier in the "Alajuela" Batallion organized after the triumph of the Liberal Revolution of 1895. And although he fought in the army of Eloy Alfaro, he was sent to the Galápagos (Floreana) for a breach of discipline.

Camilo had a naturally rebellious, independent nature and his violent temper made him a very difficult man to deal with, so that while on Floreana, he was accused of having murdered Emilio Viteri. There were, however, positive aspects to his character such as a sense of honor, and even though he was a man of few friends, he was true and generous to all. He liked his solitude and if he was treated well, could work without rest at any number of jobs.

CAMILO CASANOVA

One of Manuel J. Cobos's workers. He was exiled to Chávez Island (Indefatigable) in 1900. He was rescued after Cobos's death.

He was married to Zoila Rosa Caballero who was from Cata-rama in the province of Loja. He got along very well with his wife and during his exile, thought of her constantly and could not wait to return to her side.

Under the authority of Manuel J. Cobos, life in San Cristobal began well for Camilo. He won the sympathy of his boss who gave him the job of "bronco buster" or horse trainer because of his experience as a cavalry soldier after which he worked as a lighthouse keeper, a solitary position of relative trust. The problems began when he was made to work as a simple laborer, under a foreman's direction and at a ridiculous salary. Because of his independent personality, he could not accept spending the rest of his life working for such low wages and under such humiliating conditions and so he went from protest to boycott. Cobos could not allow such a rebellious attitude and responded with punishment which was each time more severe, 100 lashings, and then 200. This experience was to make Camilo even more intransigent, furious and bent on revenge. Everyone expected Camilo to end in desaster and he did. One day he was given 300 lashings, from which he took a while to recover, but from that point on revenge was constantly on his mind. In mid 1900, Francisco Valverde, one of Cobo's trusted foremen, found Camilo away from his assignment and severely reprimanded him. The "Manabita", a nickname for someone from the province of Manabí, got up suddenly and attacked the poor Valverde with a machete. The wounds were not fatal but left him bed-ridden for a couple of weeks. The punishment for such insolence was 400 lashings with Cobos himself present. But far from being intimidating, Camilo swore within Cobos' presence that he would end Coboss life as soon as he could. The hacienda owner could not permit such blatant insubordination and was ready to have him killed. As he could not justify a death sentence to the authorities, he decided to abandon him on Chavez Island, under the pretext that he would be completing a job for the ranch. Camilo was taken by five of his fellow workers, among them Elias Puertas. He took with him, for survival purposes, a canteen of fresh water, a blunt knife, a machete, and a small knife. His mates secretly gave him eighteen boxes of matches and some clothing.

With tears in his eyes, Camilo said goodbye to his friends. He was certain that Cobos had sent him there to die. The same workers that took him to the island gave him words of encouragement but with little conviction. There was nothing else they could do.

As the boat went farther and farther away, the figure of the unhappy Casanova remained fixed on the shore. His mind was filled with hate and foreboding. He was certainly there to die yet he longed to have his revenge on the tyrannical Cobos. All his possibilities revolved in his mind, from suicide to survival by sheer will, with the goal of someday killing his enemy. He, Camilo Casanova, could not let himself die there to be devoured by animals. He had to survive at all costs for the two things that remained in his life: vengeance and the possibility of seeing his wife again.

The first night he tried to sleep, but he found himself crying and he did not know if it was from the anger, the loneliness or the pain. He had not cried as much since he was a boy but since there were no witnesses he gave vent to his feelings and finally felt some relief.

The morning sun awoke him and upon looking at the ocean he felt totally alone. All of the same feelings of yesterday afternoon crossed his mind. He spent many long hours looking at the ocean without being able to decide on anything. He finally had a sip of water and realized that he did want to survive and that he should go look for a source of water. He was hungry but did not know what to eat. He instinctively looked for his machete and feeling it next to him, didn't know if it would defend him, help find food or be used to kill himself. In spite of all this, the presence of the machete was consoling. Since the days of his childhood in Rio Chico, he was convinced that it was his best friend and helper in life, and he was glad he knew how to use it. But where would he find something to eat? He explored the nearby area in search of food but all he could find were tortoises and iguanas. He knew that they could nourish him but first he had to overcome his aversion to eating their meat. In the end he came to enjoy the tortoise meat cooked on an open fire.

The first days were hard however. He slept close to the beach behind two high boulders, where he was visited by sea lions. Not sure he would survive, his mood went from furious to lethargic. When his water ran out he quenched his thirst with tortoise blood or with the juice of cactus or cactus fruit.

One night while he slept, the first drizzle fell, sopping his clothing which jolted him back to reality. He took shelter under a tree and used tortoise shells to cover himself. He realized he had to build a hut and started it the very next day which brought his spirits up and helped his listlessness to slowly disappear.

The following days he explored the area in search of food and fresh water: he was tired of drinking blood and the cactus water which tasted like sand paper. The land near the ocean is arid and rocky, and it took a while to find the more fertile regions which are quite a few kilometers from the beach. He explored the higher elevations but always returned to sleep on the beach. One day he decided to go farther inland, armed with his inseparable machete, axe, and a portion of turtle, he headed out on-a real exploration of the interior of the island. He visited the ravines with their green vegetation which indicated the presence of water. The sun heated up as the day wore on and his thirst made him drink from the cactus. At sundown he looked for a place to sleep so as to continue on the next day.

The island did not have many feral animals as it had never been inhabited before and so the vegetation was abundant and the going difficult. He thought about going back, but the vegetation itself indicated there had to be water somewhere close by. He came across his own tracks many times, which meant that he had been wandering around in circles. After many discouraging days of struggling through the undergrowth, he saw something that looked like a banana tree. After so many frustrations, he thought that it might be just another hallucination. He continued walking with his eyes fixed on the tree, which stood out clearly in the small stand of escalesia. As he came nearer, there was no doubt that it was a banana tree, but might it not be a sterile species found only on the islands? He continued walking forward till he could see the unmistakable green, beautiful bunches that hung from the tall stalk. With a smile on his face he began to cut them down with his machete. In a few days they would be ready and would help give his diet some variety, and the leaves would be useful in covering his hut.

In a frenzy of enthusiasm, he looked over the whole area and at each step, he found something new and amazing. There were yuca, sweet potatoes, oranges and limes all growing right in the middle of the undergrowth. In looking for an explanation, he remembered that some of the ranch workers had been exiled to the islands and among them figured Otilio Carrion, Jose Hurtado, and others. Some or all of them had left a beatiful garden which now totally changed his life. He still desperately needed water, but he was sure that he could find it somewhere in the vicinity of these healthy trees. He searched the whole area as if he were on the trail of some magnificent treasure. Hours later he found a small stream. It didn't flow abundantly but to Camilo it was the most precious water in the world. He had not had a drop in many weeks, and here was a source of the delicious liquid. Fearing that he might never find it again, he wanted to drink forever. He dunked his head again and again in the water. He wanted to feel its freshness on his face, head, feet and all over his body. He began to dance and shout for joy. Now he was sure that he would at least be able to survive for a while and that Cobos would not see him in his grave. That night he slept well after satiating himself on fruits from the garden that he had recently found.

The next day he put axe and machete to work. He needed a hut that would allow him to spend longer periods of time near his newly found paradise and a place to store the fruits of the garden.

While he was building the hut, he looked at his situation. His new hut would mainly be used for storage, and he would continue living by the beach in the hopes of being rescued by some passing

Sunset at Santa Cruz Island where Camilo Casanova spent three years of solitary (1900 - 1904)

boat. The island was beatiful and tranquil but it was still his prison and place of exile.

When he finished the shack, he had a new and happy surprise: feral chickens and roosters came to the garden to eat. It was easy to follow their tracks and find their nests and hideouts.

His situation improved daily but his main concern was to get back to the beach as soon as possible so as not to lose any opportunity of flagging down a passing boat that would take him back to civilization.

One day as he was sitting by his hut gazing at the ocean, he realized that he couldn't remember the date or even the day of the week. This alarmed him and made him realize that he could easily lose total track of time and become even more withdrawn from "civilized" ways. Thereafter, he organized his days better and spent a couple of minutes each morning carving on a tree the year 1900, on another the months and on yet another, the day. He believed that his captivity would end by the time he finished the first tree and when he was rescued he wanted to be able to count the number of days that Manuel J. Cobos had taken from him.

The matches that his friends had given him had just about run out and without fire, he couldn't prepare his food or build the bonfire to get the attention of some passing boat. He decided then that he should always have a small fire burning and lots of firewood and dead leaves on hand for that purpose.

To make his visits to his inland garden easier, he cleared out the brush and found a more direct trail which brought the hike down to less than an hour. This meant that he could leave in the morning and return that same afternoon to his place on the beach.

The months went by and he continued to watch the sea with the hope that some day a boat would appear that would take him to freedom. But for a long time, nothing happened. He could routinely see Manuel Cobos' boats on the San Cristobal-mainland route and routinely traveling between the islands, especially Isabella or Floreana, to extract tortoise oil. He knew of course that they would never come for him as long as Cobos did not allow it. Overcome with frustration and despair, he frequently vented his anger on anything that was in his way, including any of the confident birds, which having no fear of man, did not fly away on his approach.

And so ended the year 1900. At the beginning of the new year, Camilo spent long hours replanting yuca, sweet potatoes, and bananas in case his exile should continue.

His diet was extremely varied: eggs, chickens, yuca, sweet potatoes and bananas from the garden; tortoise and fish from the sea. The only thing he needed was something in place of sugar to sweeten his foods, which he succeeded in finding by using fruit juice, orange in particular, as a substitute.

His shack on the beach was comfortable, but it did not allow him a full view of the ocean which made him wonder if a passing boat could see his bonfire. A little ways away, there was a hill that was perfect for this purpose and he was amazed that he had not thought of it before. He put his axe and machete to work and spent the next couple of weeks working on his new house. His only rest was to scan the horizon in search of a sail or column of smoke from a faraway boat. His new home was big but above all it stood well above the bay allowing a complete view of the ocean and it could be seen from various viewpoints. Next to his house, he arranged everything he needed to light the bonfire which would attract the attention of visitors who would surely rescue him.

In his free time he imagined what his meeting with his rescuers would be like. It would surely be the happiest day of his life. He should always be ready and decently dressed for whenever the occasion presented itself. He realized the neccesity of keeping his hair and beard regularly trimmed as he did not want to look uncouth to his rescuers. He devised a way to use his only knife and his inseparable machete to cut hair and beard when they got too long.

He had developed a certain pattern to his activities but he still spent many hours a day just looking at the ocean. His first task was to carve the date and the day on the corresponding trees. Then he looked for firewood for cooking his food and to add to the woodpile for the bonfire which could be his salvation. Next came the more lengthy tasks, such as visiting the garden to weed, bring back provisions or to look after chickens, etc.

Around the middle of the year 1901, Camilo had returned from the garden carrying a bunch of bananas and some yuca. While he was resting in his hut, he thought he saw a slight column of smoke from a steamer that was headed towards the island. He jumped up with a start and lit the bonfire, in spite of the danger of it burning his own hut. Nothing mattered as long as he got their attention.

An elegant yacht anchored some distance from the beach, and from it a boat with a few people was lowered into the water. Some who spoke English approached his hut suspiciously at first but once they saw him were less mistrustful. Camilo did not seem to be such a dangerous criminal. He tried to make them understand with gestures hoping that his long captivity would be coming to an end. The visitors were very friendly and understanding and gave him all kinds of gifts such as cookies, crackers, matches and sweets but they would not take him off the island. When they went to say their good-byes, Camilo begged and pleaded but to no avail. He cried like a baby but the ship raised its anchors and left without him.

Some time later another yacht came to the island and the tourists were again generous and friendly to the lone inhabitant of Santa Cruz island but when it was time to go no one would take him and he was left to his solitude. Each year at the beginning of summer many yachts of the wealthy which were cruising in the Islands stopped at Santa Cruz. They visited Camilo but after a couple brief moments of hope left him lonelier and more desperate than ever with little reason to continue his unhappy existence.

And so the years 1902 and 1903 went by in the midst of daily work and illusions of liberty. He was sick many times and once gravely ill but recovered due to his strong constitution. Delirious with a high fever, he saw thousands of yachts visiting the island and his hut. In the end, with a cruel smile of rejection, they all sailed off. He dreamed that he was face to face with Cobos and confronted him with his cruelty. But the little emperor of Chatham, with the same cruel smile on his face, faded away and was lost in the crowd of tourist. Miraculously, Camilo recovered his health and returned to his life of work in the garden where he planted new fruit trees, bananas, yuca and maintained the chicken coop.

He was getting used to the solitary life and to not expect any help from any of the many foreign tourists who smiled so kindly yet in the end left him more despondent, when in the first months of 1904 he saw a different type of boat approaching the harbor. It was a ship with small canons on deck and the Ecuadorian flag waving at the stern. It anchored in front of the beach and a small boat was let down over the side. Squinting, he could barely read the name "Cotopaxi". He could not believe his eyes. It looked as if a boat belonging to the Ecuadorian navy was heading directly towards his hut. Dressed in his last rags but with dignity still, he waited for the passengers to approach him. There were various dignified and serious looking gentlemen. One of them who wore a naval uniform appeared to be the commander of the boat. On land, the four headed towards Camilo and called him by name. Camilo could barely come up with a courteous response; they knew his name, the name that no one had uttered for so many years. They had come for him and told him the reasons for his rescue. The person responsible for his banishment had died. He had been assassinated the 15th of last January. In the investigations after his death, many of the workers had spoken of those who had been banished to deserted islands and particularly of Camilo's case and so the commission had come to rescue him. The new Territorial Governor Don Juan Jose Pino, the Commander of the ship "Cotopaxi" Benigno Calderon and other representatives of the Guayaquil press were all present. He would return with them but not necessarily a free man as he still had murder charges to face for the death of Emilio Viteri on Floreana.

Camilo did not object and prepared his things to leave the island. He gathered his few belongings, offered his rescuers the fresh foods he had on hand, showed them the calendar of his solitary life etched on the trees, and boarded the small boat that would take him to the ship and the mainland.

From afar, he could see for the last time the hut that had sheltered him these last three and a half years and the elevated regions of the island where his garden and memories remained, and he boarded the boat. As the vessel was turning in the direction of the route to Guayaquil, something on a rock at the outlet of the bay caught his eye. He could see a sign clearly written in Spanish and other languages that he was not familiar with:

"Please do not take his man off the island for he is twenty times a criminal".

That was the reason then that no one would take him off the island. Cobos's cynicism was such that he was not satisfied with just sending Camilo off to live in solitary confinement but wanted to ensure that it was a permanent solution. After his initial reaction of surprise and anger, the joy of freedom overcame his feelings of vengeance which he had harbored for so many years. Besides, Cobos was dead and in the long journey back he found out the details of his tragic death.

Camilo was turned over to the authorities in Guayaquil for supposedly having assassinated Viteri. After a long investigation, he was absolved and freed.

Upon leaving jail, Camilo set out for Catarama to be reunited with his wife, but as he entered town everyone was astonished because they assumed that he had died a long time ago. This was the information that the authorities in Guayaquil had given his wife Zoila Rosa when she traveled there in search of him many years ago. "He drowned", they told her " and he didn't leave you a penny but there is a debt which you must pay". The poor woman grieved for her husband for a long time but had to accept it.

When Camilo arrived on the scene, the situation had changed and the only solution for the exiled man of Santa Cruz, was to retrace his steps and head back to Manabi. This unhappy woman ended her days filled with pain and cursed the people that had tricked her into believing that her husband, Camilo Casanova, had died.

CHAPTER VIII

MINOR –GREAT TRAGEDIES IN THE GALAPAGOS.

The Galapagos Islands, in spite of their exotic beauty, are not a good site for a shipwrecked man nor a refuge after abandoning a ship. The anguished wait for a hypothetical rescue at a time when very few ships sailed these seas or the desperation of hunger and thirst when they had arrived on a deserted island left the survivors few pleasant memories.

We have already mentioned the case of that shipwrecked man at the end of the sixteenth century who ended up turning himself into God after three years on an island.

We will never know how many ships were lost in the Archipelago or in the vicinity, but we have received news of a few, either from those who were shipwrecked themselves or from the inhabitants of the islands who rescued them.

Shipwrecks before 1832 (the year of the first settlement) obviously ended in death because of the distance and isolation of the islands. But in any case there are some exceptions, such as that of two Englishmen who arrived in Tumaco, southwest of Colombia by boat after their whaling ship, "La Josefa", sank in 1817. This case is known because of a cummunication from the Corregidor of Barbacoas to the President of the Real Audiencia of Quito, although there are no further details. The appearance of the only survivors caused great surprise and the authorities didn't know what to do in such an unusual case (1)

In 1850, the whaling ship, "La Fayette" of New Bedford was lost on Albemarle Island when she tried to anchor too close to the coast. The anchor didn't chatch on the bottom and the ship crashed against the cliffs. The wood shattered and the whaling

(1) Comm. from José Maruri to President Juan Ramírez, Oct. 16, 1817. Arch. Nac. Hist. Quito. Tumaco, Vol. 4. Fol. 175.

ship was left tilted at the mercy of the waves. Everything was lost, including 600 barrels of whale oil. The crew abandoned the ship in two boats and headed in the direction of the mainland, but they were never heard from again. The Captain and the Second officer were rescued a few days later by another whaler, the "Golconda", also from New Bedford.

Other ships escaped with serious damage after crashing against the rocks. The best known is the case of the British ship "Magicienne", which hit a rock, that was given the name of the whaler, near Gardner Bay on Hood Island.

1.— THE SHIPWRECK OF THE "BRIGANTINE AMAZONAS" 1889.

On October 5,1889, the Ecuadorian Consul's office in Panamá seemed to be undergoing an invasion of staggering spectres who, with desperately broken speech, tried to explain a tragedy and beg for help for their companions. After several repetitions, questions and clarifications, the consul was able to make out their situation.

The small brigantine, AMAZONAS, had been shipwrecked in the northern island of the Archipelago while she was fishing cod and turtles. The Captain, his family, a mate and two sailors occupied a small boat while six other crewmen were on a raft. They had managed to save some food and a little water, but they all realized that they were far from the area frequented by steamships. Fishing and rainwater helped them to survive. Their main problem was the ocean currents that carried them slowly towards the north. They streered as best they could to Cocos Island. However, they had not been able to get close enough and they were ad-vancing very slowly. They had been at the sea 19 days and the situation was becoming critical. Finally, the Captain made the only possible decision: to separate from the raft and head towards Panamá to look for help. This entailed a desperate fight against time and the currents but it was the only hope. The first days they advanced only a few miles and the two rafts remained within sight of one another. On the sixth day they sighted the far-off coast of Panamá, but thirst and hunger threatened to destroy all of their efforts. They landed at Punta Garachimi at the entrance to the Gulf and headed for the city in a desperate race with their last remaining strength. Eight days had passed since they had separated from the raft and 27 since the shipwreck..

The Ecuadorian Consul asked the Governor for assistance and, with the help of many people, the steamship "Boyacá", set sail three hours after receiving her orders. The Captain was on board to lead the search. Night fell and they had to wait until daybreak to try to locate the raft. During these slow hours they all made mental calculations about the possibility of finding the party still alive. Twenty—eight days! and if they hadn't been able to collect water, the probability was slim.

At dawn everyone scanned the horizon in search of the raft. Nothing!. The hours passed in anguish and no one left the deck although their eyes began to see shadows as a result of their fatigue. They turned to the south and then to the north following the current. The Boyacá steamed a wide circle, but nothing could be seen. When night was approaching and they were thinking of giving up the search, someone saw a dot far away in the horizon . It was the raft! When they came nearer, they were able to make out several motionless bodies lying face down. They sounded the horn desperately, trying to atract attention, but no one moved. Two were missing. Finally one man lifted his head, but let it fell again. Three of the men were alive but they were very weak. The other had died a few hours earlier. What happened to the other two? They were unable to explain. They must have fallen into the water during the night, although no one knew if they were dead or alive. They looked for them for an hour, and then they left the area because it was more urgent to save the survivors who were very weak and night was falling. So, the "Boyacá" returned to Panamá City. (1).

(1)   Communic. of N. Orfila, Consul of Panamá. Oct. 12, 1889. Arch. Nac. Hist. Quito. Min. del Interior. Vol 198.

2.– THE DESERTORS OF ALBEMARLE. 1904.

Don Antonio Gil settled on Albemarle Island in 1897 after abandoning Charles Island. He organized a plantation called "Santo Tomás", located about 20 kilometers from Puerto Villamil at the southern end of Isabela. He exploited the abundant feral (cimarron) cattle almost exclusively for their hides, raised agricultural products, rendered turtle oil and mined sulfur from one of the nearby volcanoes.

DON ANTONIO GIL

OWNER of the Hacienda Santo Tomás in the Isabela Island.

Sr. Antonio Gil.

The tortoises in the southern part of the island were considered to be the biggest and most abundant in the Archipielago. That is why Antonio Gil as well as Manuel J. Cobos of Chatham exploited them unmercifully. The writer, Nicolás Martínez, who visited the island in 1907 stated that the shells of the slaughtered tortoises covered the ponds on that part of the island and served to decorate the path up to the plantation. There were thousands of them! (1)

"LAS POZAS"

On the south of Isabela Island (Albemarle). They were full of immense tortoises at the end of the 19th century which were later exterminated.

(1) Martínez, Nic.: Impresiones de un viaje, Quito, 1911, pp. 135—142.

Santo Tomás plantation also received, as was then the custom, workers who had problems with the law. This obliged it to maintain a very strict and harsh system of control. Punishment could include the death penalty or exile to abandoned islands. Nicolás Martínez adds that more than once the two plantation owners exchanged workers for . . . cattle!

These two small empires, of Manuel J. Cobos and Antonio Gil, had grown in power and in number of inhabitants. Therefore they petitioned the goverment to obtain police and military protection. The 1901 Congress decreed the establishment of two small garrisons on the islands. About twelve soldiers arrived on Albemarle Island in 1902 and, given the distance and the lack of distractions, boredom drove them to desperation.

CISTERNS FOR WATER
The only remains of the hacienda of Don Antonio Gil on Isabela Island.

One day in 1904 eleven soldiers abandoned the camp and headed inland on the island. They didn't know the area at all, but they were convinced that they would find a way to survive and return to the mainland. They carried neither water nor supplies.

The bosses and workers of the plantation looked for them for a few days with the intention of rescuing them since they know the soldiers were headed for a certain death. They didn't find them. The soldiers had already been forgotten when, one fine day, a human figure in the last stages of exhaustion collapsed at the entrance to the plantation. It was one of the desertors.

The story of their experience was hair-raising. They had left convinced that such a big island should have villages and that some boat would take them to Guayaquil. They wandered around aimlessly for a couple of days, but then panic set in as a result of their hunger and thirst and they separated. Hallucinations drove them ever farther from one another and they never saw each other again. He was sure that all of the party were dead and eaten by the wild dogs. Nothing more was ever heard of them.

3.— ADVENTURES AND MISADVENTURES OF THE "ALEXANDER".

In 1907, there was yet another typical event in the Archipelago: the arrival of some survivors from a shipwreck who were in the last stages of exposure. In this case they were Norwegians from the sailing ship "Alexander".

They had set sail from Australia in December 1906 with 2,000 tons of coal destined for Panamá. They were trapped in the vicinity of the Galapagos by a prolonged calm which lasted more than a month. Marine currents played capriciously with the ship, taking it near Albemarle. They anchored and abandoned the boats, with the Captain and seven sailors aboard headed towards Indefatigable Island, which could be faintly seen in the distance. The second boat with the pilot and six men on board followed slightly to the east. The latter party, after rowing for several days driven by hunger and thirst, were desperate to survive when they managed

The sail boat ALEXANDER, 1907
(Stein Hoff: Drommmem om Galapagos, 1985, p. 11)
Cap. EMIL PETERSEN, SKIPPER.

to enter Puerto Chico (today Baquerizo Moreno) on Chatham Island. As the boat entered the port, it touched on a reef which broke its prow. On Chatham Island they received excellent care and recovered before being taken to Guayaquil. The writer, Nicolás Martinez, who spent some time in the Islands, was able to interview the exhausted survivors of the shipwreck and hear the details of their odyssey. (1)

Two businessmen from Guayaquil wanted to recover the "Alexander" and its cargo, so they organized an expedition guided by the Norwegian sailors. When the expedition reached the wreck they found that the old sailing ship had yielded to the dashing of the sea and weather. All that could be seen of it were the dark masts. Disappointed, they returned to the mainland.

What had happened to the Captain and his companions?

Almost a year later a ship left Guayaquil to look for them, following the directions of the pilot who had seen them disappear behind Indefatigable Island. They were found safe and sound. They had survived thanks to the tortoises, the goats, the vegetation of the island and water they found a short distance from the coast. One of the sailors had died of illness, but the survivors who were in good condition, were taken to Chatham where they were treated like kings.

4.— THE TRAGEDY OF THE "TOMASITA". 1908

Don Antonio Gil Quesada had taken charge of the Santo Tomás plantation after his father became too old to carry on. Leather, turtle oil and sulfur production were increasing and they maintained active commerce with Guayaquil using two sloops. One of them, the "TOMASITA", was commanded by Captain Chiapella, an Italian who had settled on the plantation with his family.

The "Tomasita" was sailing around the north end of the Al-

(1) Martínez Nicolás: Op. Cit. pp. 178-80.

bemarle in 1908 when she foundered on an unknown rock, which opened a hole in the hull. She sank within a few minutes. Captain Chiapella had his wife and his small son with him, as well as several workers.

They were all able to swim ashore, but they were far from the plantation.

The workers set out along the coast to Santo Tomás, but it was impossible to advance rapidly over the lava outcrops, the dense vegetation and the difficult terrain of the shore. Hunger and thirst brought them near death, but they reached the plantation on their last legs and gave the news to Don Antonio Gil. A sloop set sail immediatelly to rescue Captain Chiapella and his party but ten days had passed since the accident. When the rescuers arrived, they found that Captain, his wife and his son had all died of thirst. Certain details of the bodies allow them to imagine the last hours of that terrible drama. The last one to die must have been the small child. A heroic but useless effort of paternal love.

5.— THE SHIPWRECK OF THE "ALBATROS". 1927.

James Island (Santiago) has a rich salt mine that was discovered in the past century, although it was not systematically exploited until the 1920's. In 1926, the salt was analyzed and its quality was found to be superior to that extracted in Santa Elena, west of Guayaquil, for the consumption on the mainland. The reserves were calculated at more than a million hundred-weight.

Salt exploit began sporadically. This commerce was carried out in coordination with other jobs of the settlers on the Islands.

In 1926, the United Maritime Society of Guayas was formed in Guayaquil to encourage navigation and commerce towards the Galapagos. They acquired the schooner "ALBATROS" to make regular voyages to the Islands for the purpose of exploiting the salt on a large scale.

The "Albatros" made her maiden voyage the same year, although she also had to look for and attempt to rescue the crew from a Pailebot "Cesar" which had been shipwrecked near James Island.

The schooner fulfilled her mission, even though then the ship-wrecked men who had taken refuge in the shacks of the salt mine had been picked up by the small steamship "Cañon" which was passing through the Archipelago. The schooner "Albatros" loaded up with salt and returned to Guayaquil.

After several voyages her turn came.

The "Albatros" left Guayaquil on January 26, 1927, under the command of Captain Jorge Morlas who had been a naval officer, carrying 16 passengers in addition to the crew. They loaded several tanks of petroleum which were placed on the deck without the necessary precautions. Three hundred miles from the coast on January 28 an uncontrolable fire broke out and destroyed everything. Only three sailors who had been able to lower a lifeboat and escape from that hell were saved. A few days later they were picked up by a ship and taken to Panamá. The fact that three sailors were saved without a scratch, when there were various passangers and children aboard the ship caused all kinds of commentaries in which fantasy played a major role. The sailors were detained when they returned from Panamá, but they were later acquited of all charges. It was a long time before the emotions of relatives and fiends were calmed.

The "United Maritime Society" had received a blow, morally and economically, from which they were unable to recover.

6.— NORWEGIANS IN THE GALAPAGOS (1926—1928)

The Archipelago was a point of attraction for Scandinavians and especially for Norwegians beginning in the middle of the past century. We do not know if this was because of their adventurous spirit or sailors' reports, but from the decade of the 1870's we find various records of exploratory talks with the Ecuadorian

Government regarding colonization of the Islands.

The acceptance of these proposals was so widespread that Adolfo Beck had August F. Christensen draw up a very detailed map of Charles Island in 1881.

The only difficulty was the claim made by the descendants of José de Villamil for possession of that island.

In 1885 the Congress passed special legislation for the administration of the Archipelago (it was no longer a separate province but governed by Guayaquil). But it expressly stated:

> "The former disposition does not prejudice the rights of the Compañía Suizo-Escandinava to colonize the Galapagos, according to the contract of August 8, 1884".

Adolf Beck informed the Ecuadorian Goverment of the forthcoming arrival of a good number of Norwegian immigrants, stating that they were "excellent sailors, famous fishermen and very good laborers, and I am satisfied that they are the most appropiate for the colonization of the islands".

He requested an extension of the contract to facilitate the immigration of the group and the suppression of the clause that imposed Ecuadorian nationality. President Caamaño's goverment accepted the first petition, but refused to concede the second. Thus the enterprise was disolved. It was too difficult to renounce one's nationality before seeing the reality and possibilities of success.

In spite of everything, the Galapagos Islands must have remained in the memories of many Norwegians because 30 years later we find them in conversation with the government again. This time it was August F. Christensen himself who headed the project to form an enterprise for exploitation of the fishing by means of industrial production of canned and salted fish, the capture of whales as well as agriculture and ranching on Charles and Indefatigable Islands.

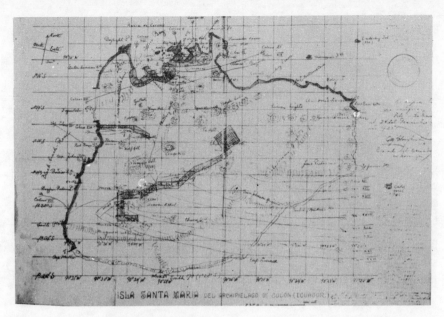

FLOREANA ISLAND WHERE THE FIRST ATTEMPTS OF FORMAL COLONIZATION TOOK PLACE (MAP OF A. CHRISTENSEN 1925).

AUGUST F. CRISTENSEN: the main promoter of the Norwegian colonization of Galapagos. (S. Hoff: Drommem om Galapagos, 1985, p. 18)

"CASA MATRIZ" or main center of the Norwegian colony on Floreana. 1926.
(S. Hoff: Drommen om Galapagos, 1985)

The new Norwegian colony of Santa Cruz Island. 1927. (S. Hoff: Drommen om Galapagos, 1985, p.122)

The first contracts were signed in 1925.

The arrival of some 40 colonists who would settle in Post Office Bay and Black Beach on Charles Island was announced for March, 1926. There they built a big wooden house ("Casa Matriz") and a fishing and whaling center.

The presence of this group of Norwegians caused a lot of expectation in Ecuador because it was the first experiment with European colonization in the present century, and it was carried out by people who had already achieved prestige as great fishermen.

The arrival of a second group composed of 30 families, some 80 people, was announced for December of the same year. They came from Panamá in the schooner "Albemarle". They settled temporarily on Chatham and from there they went on to Indefatigable. Unfortunately, while this group was building its first houses, the news arrived that the Charles Island colony had disintegrated and was returning to their homeland.

In June, 1927, a new contract with the "Sociedad Anonima de Santa Cruz" represented by Thomas Vaag was ready. It was never ratified because the colony had begun to abandon the island. "La Sociedad . . ." was officially declared dissolved in December of that same year.

In June 1928 some thirty colonists still remaining in the Galápagos approached the government to request a loan of a million sucres to salvage the initial project, or, if that were not possible, the purchase of their remaining equipment. The request was signed by Axel Seeberg. President Isidro Ayora, after receiving the reports about the condition of the equipment and the hopelessness of stabilizing the colony, denied both petitions.

Some of the equipment had not yet been installed and some of it was deteriorated from exposure to the weather and the voyage.

In July, 1930, August F. Christensen was still trying to save what was left by selling their interests to the Van Camp Company of California, but Ecuador didn't accept this sale because some clauses had not been complied with and the contract foresaw that any transfer of assets could only be accomplished with a company with Norwegian capital. Much of the equipment was seized by the Ecuadorian Government under an embargo.

There has been a lot of guessing as to the reasons for the failure of the Norwegians in the Galápagos. The difference in the climate, the lack of capital, the distance to markets, the scarcity of water, and even the psychological problems of a colony made up almost exclusively of men which was not helpful for the adaptation to such a different and difficult environment, were all contributing factors.

More than one of these reasons can be seen in the communication sent by the head of the Charles Island Colony, Axel Seeberg to the Ecuadorian government in June, 1928:

> "The failure of our enterprise is due to several factors among them I will mention that our organizers totally lacked in experience in these Ecuadorian Islands.
>
> They painted such an easy and simple picture of everything in reference to plantations, fishing, whale hunting, etc. that hundred of good Norwegians were tricked and today find themselves with no means of subsistence. This is why the colonists have lost everything they had, realizing too late that they were victims of the organizers' hoax. This would not have happened if, before trying to colonize the Islands, the organizers had sent an expedition of serious men who knew the terrain and could appreciate the good and bad possibilities . . .
>
> It has cost us an enormous quantity of money to find an adequate method for salting, drying and preserving the different fish, taking into account that this job is performed in a very hot climate, just the opposite of the cold that we are accustomed to in our homeland.

Whale hunting on a small scale is also possible with the help of an adequate boat and a station on the island. In the same way it is possible to use the meat of the enormous wild cattle to our advantage. Today the meat of these herds is lost.

To achieve this, the enterprise needs, in round numbers, a million sucres. . .

In the islands there are still some thirty colonists, who lived miserably; some from fishing and others from their crops. They all have a very good experience acquired during these years of trial, disappointment and suffering. . .

If the Government does not accept this project, or resolves that it cannot invest in these islands, I hope, in the name of all of us, that you will buy everything we have on Charles and Indefatigable Islands, for a quantity that would allow us to return to our homeland with at least a small part of the money we have invested and in consideration of the profitless year we have spent here. I repeat that we are all in disastrous situation, especially those of us who are married and have wives with no means of subsistence in our homeland . . ."

This ended another attempt to colonizing the Archipelago, although it managed to preserve the ecological future of the islands. Axel Seeberg died two months later in Quito.

Some of the Norwegians, however, decided to remain in this area and ended up settling in the Archipelago or in other parts of the country where they also served as a link with those who had some interest in the islands. We will mention some of them: Captain Bruun and Trygve Nuggerud, whose lives ended tragically as we shall soon see, and others such as A. Worm-Muller, Knut Arends, Haense, etc. . .

Captain Paul Bruun: in 1911, skipper of the steam ship "Neptun",

(Stein Hoff: Drommem om Galapagos, 1985, p. 56)

7.— THE DEATH OF CAPTAIN BRUUN. 1931.

Captain Bruun was very well known in the islands and for some time he wanted to refloat the colonization project. His past is filled with legends and mysterious pages. It was said that he was a paid spy for the German Naval Intelligence Service during the First World War and as such, was responsible for sinking the English ship "Hampshire", which was torpedoed by a submarine. His arrival in Guayaquil was also surrounded by mysteries, since he arrived with no documents, adducing that he had been shipwrecked and had lost everything. In 1929, while he was trying to run the colony, he was also in charge of commanding the "Manuel J. Cobos" the only ship that made voyages between the islands and the mainland.

The small colony still had the small yacht "NORGE" at its disposal for hunting cattle on various islands, fishing and trade. At the end of 1931, the "Norge" without gasoline aground in Iguana Cove at the southwest end of Isabela. Captain Bruun and his sailors walked back to Puerto Villamil to get gaso - line. Since the "Manuel J. Cobos" was anchored in the port, it took them back to the site of the accident. It couldn't come too close because of the rock outcrops, so Captain Bruun and four companions continued the trip to the "Norge" which could be seen about two miles away, with the gasoline in a small boat called "chalana".

From the "Cobos", Knut Arends saw them sailing away and when he thought that they no longer needed help, he went on to Indefatigable.

When the small vessel was heading towards its destination and almost alongside the "Norge", misfortune occurred. The sea was rough and the boat was overloaded. A wave caused the boat to become unbalanced and one of the crew lost on oar. When he tried to recover it, the boat tilted dangerously at the same time a wave rushed in. . The crew threw themselves into the water and tried to reach the beach, except Captain Bruun who continued fighting to save the boat and its contents. When the men reached

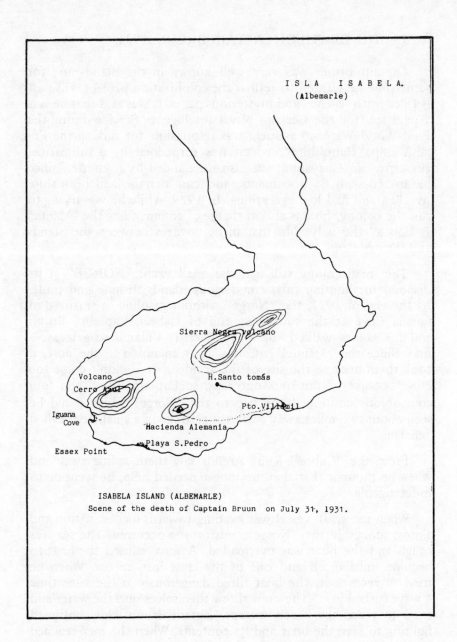

ISLA ISABELA.
(Albemarle)

Sierra Negra volcano

Volcano
Cerro Azul

H.Santo tomás

Iguana
Cove

Pto.Villamil

Hacienda Alemania

Playa S.Pedro

Essex Point

ISABELA ISLAND (ALBEMARLE)
Scene of the death of Captain Bruun on July 31, 1931.

the beach, the Captain did not appear. Hours later he was found dead among the rocks on San Pedro Beach. Probably he had received a hard blow on the head which made him lose consciousness and fall into the water and drown.

Since is was impossible to carry the corpse to Puerto Villamil more than 40 kilometers away over terrible lava fields, they decided to bury him there, leaving a rough wooden cross made from the remains of the "chalana" as marker.

The walk to the Port across the lava fields took several days and the men almost collapsed from hunger and thirst. Even before they arrived, Knut Arends, who had heard no news from Captain Bruun decide to find out for himself what had happened. With a crew of four he headed out to see in a small launch named "Pinta". At Essex Point, very near Iguana Cove, they anchored the launch to continue the trip on foot. Once again, the sea levied its tribute. A strong wave broke the anchor rope and flung the small vessel against the rocks. Arends and his companions were saved by a miracle. They were able to recover some provisions and then visited the "Norge". Since they found no one there, they took the road back towards Santo Tomás. Arends and two young workers went ahead to ask for help and to find out what had happened to Captain Bruun. The other two, named Avelino and Rugel, were unable to follow at the same pace because of their age and fell behind.

Several workers set out from the plantation immediately and found Avelino almost unconscious, but Rugel didn't appear anywhere. Avelino remembered that two nights before they had fallen asleep together, but when he woke up at dawn, Rugel had disappeared. They looked for him for several days, but without any results.

The "Norge" was refloated, but the small Norwegian colony which was still struggling to survive in the islands received a heavy blow from the death of Captain Bruun and ended up dispersing. Knut Arends and Trygve Nuggerud played a part in the drama on Charles Island and in the disappearance of the Baroness as we shall see in the next chapter.

CHAPTER IX.

PUZZLES AND CRIMES.

The German Colony on Floreana
and the Mystery of the Baroness.

Preamble

Our story begins in 1924 with the publication of William Beebe's book, "Galapagos, World's End" which was to change the traditional image of the Islands. From their discovery in 1535, the impression of the islands was fairly gloomy: an inhospitable place, good only for pirates and whalers who would stop to take on provisions of fresh meat and water. William Beebe's book altered this picture drastically as he painted the Galapagos as a place of primitive beauty, worthy of study and preservation.

Coincidentally, in that same year, 1924, a group of Norwegian adventurers was planning to emigrate to the Archipelago to establish a colony and fish the rich waters of the islands. The project failed, but the news of the reality of life in the Galapagos Islands spread through various countries.

On the other hand, Europe was living through a period of selfdoubt when the values of western civilization were being questioned and many were to turn to a simple, natural, primitive life. The Galapagos Islands would be an ideal spot for such life, perhaps because they lay on the other side of the world. Germany was one of the countries most affected and many Germans emigrated to different places far from Europe. One group went to Floreana Island in the Galapagos and another, the Angermeyers, to Santa Cruz Island in addition to other sporadic visitors.

FROM BERLIN TO FLOREANA. 1929.

On the night of July 3, 1929, the S.S. Boskoop set sail

from Amsterdam for America. On the deck of the transatlantic steamer two figures stood together, watching as the lights of the port and then the coast of Europe faded into the distance. It was a warm summer night and they stood there for several hours without talking, even though the same memories, thoughts and plans were going through their minds. They had just abandoned Berlin, presumably forever and left Europe with its tired civilization behind.

The memories that they hoped to erase were not pleasant ones: two failed marriages, frustrated hopes and an endless number of unflattering memories. In the following days they hoped to recover from the exhaustion and emotion of the last few months in which they had made millions of plans and acquired countless items which would help them begin their new life on a solitary island in the Pacific on the other side of the world.

The two figures were Doctor Friedrich Ritter and Dora Strauch, two very different people in age and temperament, brought together by a strange desire to change the failure of their lives through a new contact with nature. The lights of Europe disappeared and with them the memory of their bitter experiences.

Friedrich Ritter was born in Wollbach in the Black Forest around the year 1886. He did not have fond memories of his childhood because of his father's harsh temper. From that time he was quiet and solitary, seeking peace by going off into the wilderness of the forest. After finishing high school, he entered the University of Freiburg where he studied chemistry, physics, philosophy and medicine.

When he was twenty, he married Mila Clark, a student of vocal music, whom, for a time, he helped to finish her studies and begin her professional career. When war was declared in 1914, Friedrich enlisted in the army and fought in the trenches and artillery. After the Armistice in 1918, he returned to the university where he graduated as a Doctor of Odontology even though his passion was Philosophy. Upon moving to Berlin his problems began, curiously enough, because of Mila's decision to abandon her career to dedicate more time to her home.

Dora Strauch was in Berlin at this same time. She was married to a school teacher by the name of Körwin who was twice her age (she was 23 and he 45). Dora's romantic spirits and artistic tastes clashed with Herr Körwin's narrow and uncreative mentally. Multiple sclerosis caused her to limp and prevented her from having children, which was her dream in life. Her illness was what put her in contact with Dr. Ritter, who was working at the Hydrotherapeutic Institute of Berlin. Dora was fascinated with the doctor's philosophy, his enthusiasm for Nietzsche and his desire to return to "nature" to become a new Robinson Crusoe as in the novel by Gottfried Schnabel "Die Insel Felsenburg". (1) Friedrich and Dora, not at all happy in their marriages, began to dream of a new life far from European civilization and began to look for the ideal place to fulfill their desires.

For two years they lived as lovers, all the while maintaining a double life. Friedrich was the difficult and cold husband who made Mila's life intolerable, and Dora was a bank employee and school teacher's housewife, all the while preferring her role as the enthusiastic disciple of the eccentric philosopher, Dr. Ritter.

Reading William Beebe's and Schnabel's books led them to the decision to leave Europe and begin a new life in the Galapagos. At the same time, Friedrich and Dora's love affair was no longer a secret to their respective spouses and to avoid more problems and scandals, they tried to convince them to accept a salomonic solution; that upon leaving for the Galapagos, their spouses, would not only accept their decision but would themselves unite in marriage.

(1) Schnabel's novel "Die Inseln Felsenburg" describes four exiles who abandon civilization in favor of a primitive Paradise. They leave their ship and take refuge in an old pirates' cave. They eventually settle in a small volcanic valley with a stream and ravine in the middle of the island. Curiously enough, the novel ends with a murder and suicide.

Preparation for the trip was not easy but they devoted all their energies to the task. Friedrich was to get all that was necessary for life on a primitive island such as tools, construction materials, all sorts of containers, and of course his favorite philosophy books. Dora was to gather kitchen and sewing supplies, bed linens, and stainless steel dishes, etc. The Doctor decided that they would take very little medicine as they believed more in the power of the mind over illness than in treatment with drugs.

In June of 1929, Friedrich had all his teeth extracted and gave up his job to prepare for their journey.. A couple days before leaving for Amsterdam, they organized a small party to which a few friends were invited. It was supposedly organized so that their spouses could meet each other. Only their most intimate friends knew that it was a good-by party. The voyage to the New World and the unknown seemed like a honeymoon with the illusion of rebuilding their lives according to the ideals of the new "Robinson Crusoe of the Galapagos".

On July 10, the Azores were sighted, and even though their primary destination had been the Galapagos, they had not given up the possibility of settling on the Azores due to its climate, tranquility and closeness to Europe, where they could easily get books. But, as soon as they got off the boat, they changed their minds when they believed that capitalist and Jewish emmigrants, fleeing the revolutions in Europe, had flocked to the island seeking a secure haven.

On July 20, they continued their trip to Curacao, Balboa, Panamá and finally, the Pacific Ocean, arriving in Guayaquil on August 3rd. One month of navigation had put them on the other side of the world, far from their past and with hopes of beginning the new life which they had dreamed of.

The next trip to the Galapagos on the only boat that covered this route was set for the end of the same month, so they took this opportunity to travel inland. They went by train to Riobamba and from there took a bus to Quito where they stayed for several days visiting the city and climbing the Pichincha volcano.

On August 31, they set sail from Guayaquil on the ship "Manuel J. Cobos" under the command of the Norwegian captain Bruun.. They found themselves again at sea on the last stage of their voyage. From their conversations with the Captain, they tried to get more exact information about the islands to compare with their impressions, which were taken solely from books. Captain Brunn knew the island's potential as he was a member of the Norwegian expedition that had attempted to colonize the islands just three years before. Dr. Ritter's idealized vision of Floreana would be revised before he arrived.

The first view of Floreana was not particularly impressive because of the grayness of the "escalesia" trees, and the cactus and lava flows which lend both a feeling of mystery and disenchantment.

On arriving at the beach, the travelers came across the only inhabitant of the island, a young man named Hugo who, under the orders of Captain Bruun, spent periods on the island hunting the wild cattle. With Hugo's help, they unloaded some boxes but decided to accept the Captain's invitation to visit the other islands of the Archipelago. They were to return to settle on Floreana on September 19,1929.

The work of unloading the rest of the boxes, packages, equipment, and tools was no easy task and took all day. Finally, at nightfall, they found themselves watching as the little boat, their only tie to civilization, sailed away from the island. When the boat disappeared, they looked for a place to spend the night and found lodgings in the houses abandoned by the Norwegians.

The next day, with the help of Hugo who was familiar with all the trails on the island, they set out to explore it. As the boy's job was to hunt cattle on the island, he fired on the first bull he came across. Dr. Ritter was furious. Using gestures and the few words he knew in Spanish, he severely reprimanded Hugo, not so much for having killed the bull but for having eaten its meat which he considered a sin. Friedrich was a vegetarian.

After a few hours, they came across some pirate caves. They

"MANUEL J. COBOS" the everlasting boat. It was still sailing in 1934.

(Stein Hoff: Drommen om Galapagos, 1985, p. 141

were relatively comfortable and there were many signs of previous use, so they decided to spend the night in one of them.

Continuing their exploration the following day, they came across a crater with a fresh water spring which, together with the cave, evoked the description of the island found in Schnabel's novel. It was the ideal spot and they decided to settle there. Dora would remember, years later, Friedrich's exact words: "This is our place and we'll call it Friedo. In the name of the Ritters, I take possession of you, beautiful valley, against all intruders and I baptize you with this pure water, Friedo, our garden of peace". On the other hand, Hugo did not want to sleep there because he knew that a man had died there and he was afraid that his ghost would still be haunting the area.

Friedrich and Dora found a place for themselves under the acacia tree and tried to sleep, but within a few hours they realized they were not the only ones there. The underbrush was coming alive and from all sides you could hear mooing, barking and all kinds of noise. It was the feral animals that were abundant on the island.

September 22nd was the most difficult day and the one that Dr. Ritter's companion would not forget. It was the day they moved all their belongings, brought from Europe and Guayaquil, and the day in which Dora saw for the first time the difficult and uncaring side of Friedrich. They had to make countless trips on narrow trails through lava and dwarf "escalesia" forests to carry the dozens of boxes and packages to their destination. Hugo's help and that of an old horse was invaluable. For Dora, it was demoralizing to see Friedrich's indifference and hardness towards her. The honeymoon was over and there was a widening distance between them that would just get worse with time.

By the beginning of October, they had finished their move, started a garden and began construction of a house. Everything was improving except for Dr. Ritter's mood which left Dora totally distressed. Around this time Captain Bruun came to see how they were doing and to deliver the mail. When he left, he took Hugo with him which meant that the island was now left exclusively to the new arrivals. The earth began to produce, but the green of the garden also attracted competitors, the ants and wild animals, which visited it day and night.

Daily chores were intense, but they knew that their future depended upon it. They rose at dawn, that is to say when the chirping of the birds replaced the nocturnal racket of the feral donkeys, pigs, cats, dogs and cows. Friedrich picked fresh fruit for their breakfast, after which each one began the most pressing tasks. Freidrich cut down trees and cleared land for cultivation and built a house. Dora took care of the chickens and plants in the little garden. At noon, they ate their second and last meal, after which they rested until three or four in the afternoon, especially when the heat was unbearable. During these afternoon hours, Friedrich read or wrote while Dora sewed or wrote. When it cooled off, they would go back to work until sunset.

At night, Friedrich worked on his philosophical writings and read out loud while Dora made rugs or mats out of banana leaves. By eight or nine o'clock at night, Dora was asleep. Friedrich was in the habit of going out to collect cockroaches and other insects that fed on his plants and that, at the same time, could be fed to the chickens.

Friedrich was very strict in his diet and lifestyle, which made Dora bitter. While he stated that he was a vegetarian, there were periods when he went off his diet. He also excluded all kinds of flours from his diet because he believed that mankind's decadence was due to the harmful affects; therefore bread was completely eliminated from his diet.

In spite of the hard work and Dr. Ritter's harshness, February, March, and April of 1930 were the happiest and most tranquil months for Dora. In adapting to the island, they could see that not only could they live well but they were certain that the birds and feral beasts would be their only companions on the islands. It is possible that this freedom, along with the unknown presence of a visitor on the island, started the rumors that they lived like Adam and Eve in Paradise.

In May 1930, the "Manuel J. Cobos" arrived with mail from Germany. The newspaper were filled with sensationalistic articles recounting the flight of Dr. Ritter and his lover all the way to the Galapagos. They felt as if they had been discovered. They had the feeling that their long sought after anonymity was gone forever, and they thought of how this would be affecting their families at home.

So their dream of complete solitude on a deserted island had vanished. Soon visitors would arrive to see the new Adam and Eve in Paradise in the Galapagos; the much feared journalists and worst of all, the imitators and followers of their idyllic lifestyle.

The first visitors were some Norwegians who had not left the islands after their business failed in 1927. Captain Bruun, Arthur Wôrm-Muller and Knud Arends came, accompanied by an English doctor, with the intention of starting up their business again, making use of the old abandoned buildings. This time they would concentrate exclusively on fishing and hunting cattle. A short time later, five young Germans arrived, one of whom was a woman, who thought that they could live in this idyllic corner of the world.

For Dr. Ritter the presence of the "intruders" was introlerable, while for Dora it was a nice change. She seemed very enthusiastic about the presence of these good looking men with whom she could talk and exchange ideas. She could not mask her enthusiasm, and the impression that she left on the visitors was that of a very vivacious woman. This was distasteful to Dr. Ritter.

The stay of the intruders was short, happily for Friedrich. The young Germans quickly realized that they had no calling for the life of a Robinson Crusoe on a deserted island and they left. The one benefit that the Ritters received from their visit was the gift of a sweet little burro who was adored by Dora and consequently became the source of new arguments with Friedrich.

DORA AND FRIEDRICH ON FLOREANA

DORA STRAUCH AND HER PET "FLECK" on FLOREANA

The Norwegians withdrew after the tragic death of Captain Bruun whose small boat capsized. During the summer, millionaires would arrive on their yachts for short periods of time, mainly to meet the unusual couple. The one who was most famous and the closest to the tragic events on the Galapagos was the California millionaire, Allan Hancock, whose fortune came from real estate sales in Hollywood. Hancock's first visit to the Galapagos took place in January, 1932, on his yacht. He came accompanied by some biologists as his trips had a certain scientific bent to them. One of these scientists has left us some interesting observations on the strange inhabitants of Floreana.

Allan Hancock and his companions got off the boat and followed the narrow trails in search of the Ritters. "After a long and hot walk, Garth tells us, we heard the little donkey's bugle call, which got Dr. Ritter out of bed immediately, followed by Dora, still in her nightgown. Both seemed very happy to see us, even though Dora was much more lively and communicative. After the initial greetings in English and German, we sat under two large plum trees. The abundance and excellent quality of the fruit was noticed by all. Besides the plums covering the ground which we tread on with each step, there were many kinds of bananas, papayas, limes, watermelons, sugarcane, coconuts, corn, tobacco, sweet potatoes, tomatoes and other vegetables".

Dr. Ritter showed them, not without pride, an ingenious mechanism he had devised for grinding sugar cane. Dora showed off her cats, which were very useful for capturing birds, whose feathers were collected for stuffing pillows. When the visit was over, Hancock invited them to an evening of music on his yacht. It was a memorable evening for both.

John Hancock, wanting to be generous with the new Adam and Eve, asked them what they needed before he set sail. Friedrich asked only for oil for his lamps, while Dora, under Hancock's insistent queries, ended up asking for soap and flour, in spite of Friedrich's clear opposition. Her resistance gone, she ended up accepting rice, chocolate, cooking oil and coffee, again without the Doctor's consent. According to Garth, they had enough food for a year. As last good—by gift and to appease Friedrich, Allan gave him a beautiful Winchester rifle and various boxes of bullets and he gave Dora an oven.

The journalists' impertinence was even more difficult to take, not only because of their sensationalism but also because of their offers to pay Dr. Ritter and Dora for articles. With visitors to the island and in published articles alike, Dr. Ritter wanted to leave the impression of a man guided by a new philosophy in search of a simple and primitive life, in harmony with nature and his fellow human beings. That is how he presented himself in an interview with an official of the Ecuadorian Navy that was published in the "El Telegrafo" newspaper in Guayaquil.

However, his efforts were not always successful because inconsistencies in his strict vegetarian diet and his cruel treatment of Dora were obvious.

"VELERO III" The yatch of Allan Hancock in Floreana

THE LOVERS OF FLOREANA
Dora and Freidrich on board *the Velero III*
in January 1932

THE WITTMER FAMILY ON FLOREANA
Heinz had Rolf in his arms, Harry and
Margaret.

Dora's, in spite of her admiration for her lover's philosophy and her acceptance of woman's complete subjugation to man, could not accept his arbitrariness in other area, such as his contempt for her love of flowers for which she had a passion since she was a child, his constant recriminations regarding her affection for the little donkey, and his rejection of certain foods that contained flour and his total prohibition of bread.

Dr. Ritter never wrote about his disagreements with Dora but, as an enthusiastic follower of Nietzsche for whom "the contempt for women is the first ethical rule of the philosopher", it is certain that the "perfect harmony" he repeatedly mentions in so many of his articles was a simple disguise to hide the confusing reality of life on Friedo.

2. THE NEW AND PERMANENT INTRUDERS
August 1932.

Dr. Ritter and Dora had occasionally sent articles and communiques to German and English newspapers which published their work enthusiastically. In these writings an idyllic vision of life on Floreana appeared. The repercussion of these articles was unforeseen and would later come back to haunt the first colonists of the island. Soon, followers and imitators appeared with the hope of abandoning civilization and returning to a simple life in a primitive environment.

At the end of August, 1932, Friedrich and Dora could see a small sailboat attempting to approach the island. Unfortunately, it succeeded and two men and a woman, helped by three sailors,, got off the boat. It was filled with boxes, packages, two Alsatian dogs and some chickens. They were shocked to see this because it meant that the intruders were here to stay. After the short stays of the Germans and the Norwegians, they were not at all enthusiastic about having new neighbors who would take away their privacy. They had heard rumors that new Europeans would be coming, but they had held on to the hope that it was just rumor or at least that would only visit for a short time.

The new arrivals, also German, were following in Friedrich and Dora's footsteps, not only because they had been inspired by W. Beebe's books but also because they had read Dr. Ritter's articles. Their names were Heinz and Margarita Wittmer and their 12 year old son Harry. Heinz was the secretary of the Burgermeister of Cologne, Conrad Adenauer, and the idea of living in the Galapagos had come to him during Christmas of 1931 after reading an article by Dr. Ritter. They were a middle—aged couple who agreed that they wanted to give their sickly son a more healthy life. An island in the middle of the ocean seemed a perfect place.

All their savings went to buying everything they could imagine needing on an island, and they threw themselves into the adventure. They left Amsterdam in July and arrived in Guayaquil at the beginning of August 1932 and shortly thereafter landed on the island of San Cristobal, but from there it was difficult finding transportation to Floreana. After waiting a long while, the governor of the islands arranged for a small sail boat, and with the help of three sailors, they set sail. This final leg of the journey was to be a true odyssey. As they arrived in front of the island, they were dragged by the wind and current to Isabella. On the third day, after enormous effort, they were finally able to reach their destination.

Transferring the countless boxes and packages to the beach was a hopeless task as the boat could not get close enough to shore without getting destroyed. They were finally alone, just as the Ritters had been three years before, without knowing where to begin. Heinz and Margarita's personalities were such that they could overcome difficulties and even in the midst of problems, they could still find time to enjoy the details of life. Heinz was middle-aged, somewhat bald, hard-working and friendly. Margarita was much younger, very attractive and practical. Harry was frail but animated. The two Alsatian dogs completed the family.

Their first meeting with the Ritters was not particulary pleasant, even though it might be thought that the arrival of another couple would be a welcome change from the normal solitude of the islands. In the long conversation of that first afternoon, they studied each other and came to conclusions about their future relationship. The news from Germany, the tastes of each one and the possible connections in the homeland were all minutely analyzed. In the conversation Margarita expressed that one of the reasons for choosing Floreana had been the presence of a doctor on the island, which did not sit well with either Friedrich or Dora. Margarita was in her fifth month of pregnancy.

The Wittmers spent their first night in a tent near the beach, but the next morning Heinz and Harry set out to explore the interior of the island until they arrived at the pirate caves which were a couple hours from the beach. The place seemed like a good, temporary refuge and they enthusiastically returned to Margarita. She had a delicious meal awaiting them.

The following day, they began to move the boxes and, even though the place did not look as comfortable as she had imagined it, it was next to a spring of pure water. While Heinz and Harry picked fruit from the nearby trees, papayas, limes, oranges, the ever practical Margarita transformed the caves into a warm home. To make their day complete, a bull crossed their path and was killed by Heinz's sure shot.

By nightfall, the Wittmer family felt satisfied at having started a new life and bold adventure on the right foot. They looked with pride at their new, improvised home in the cave which was illuminated by the sun as it set behind the volcanoes of Isabella island. Behind them was Germany, perhaps forever, as they felt they had found a new country in this corner of the world. They came with the intention of staying and from that moment forward, they acted with that thought in mind.

Moving all the boxes, packages, and household goods was exhausting and took several days. The Ritter's coldness was obvious and only worsened when the Wittmers asked to borrow Dora's little donkey. From that day on Margarita and Dora's accounts of what happened on Floreana would be increasingly opposite.

Given the abundance of fruits and animals, surviving on the islands would not be difficult. All it took was an hour and one could come back with a week's worth of pork or beef, while all kinds of fruit were there for the taking. But the work of the first couple of months of clearing the lands for cultivation, for the garden, for the chicken coop and the future house was extremely tough. Besides, they soon found that the abundance brought on other headaches: it attracted uninvited guests. Heinz and Margarita always had a firearm or machete on hand to scare off meddlesome animals that could finish off weeks of work in a few brief seconds.

THE PIRATES' CAVE
in Floreana.

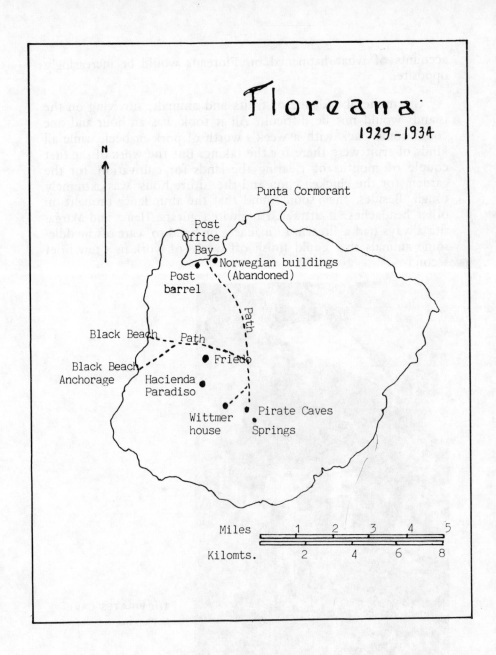

Floreana
1929-1934

N

Punta Cormorant

Post Office Bay

Norwegian buildings
(Abandoned)

Post barrel

Path

Black Beach   Path

Black Beach
Anchorage

Friedo

Hacienda
Paradiso

Wittmer
house

Pirate Caves

Springs

Miles   1   2   3   4   5

Kilomts.   2   4   6   8

3.— THE MYSTERIOUS INTRUDERS: THE BARONESS
October 1932

The Wittmers had not even had a chance to get settled on Floreana before the arrival of some other Germans on the island was announced. It happened in October, according to Margarita's diary, in November according to Dora. The word spread that a group of visitors had installed themselves in Post Office Bay. The news had a disturbing note to it: all the letters had been opened! By whom? They would soon know.

The Baroness and three companions had settled in the houses abandoned by the Norwegians on Post Office Bay. They brought with them an incredible amount of baggage which disturbed the inhabitants of Floreana even more, as it meant that they were here to stay.

The appearance of the Baroness on "Friedo" was a surprise. She came riding a donkey with her three companions following behind. Dora would later remember their arrival. "She was a slender small woman with platinum blonde hair. Her most distinctive feature was her wide, red mouth, with protruding teeth. She wore dark glasses, a type of work overall, sandals on her feet, and a beret on her head."

All were impressed with her title of Baroness and there was no doubt that she knew how to act like one. Once again, Dr. Ritter and Dora's writings about their life on the Galapagos had their effect: they had served as an open invitation to invade the island.

Stranger still was the group of men that had formed around the Baroness, two Germans and one Ecuadorian, all of whom seemed dependent on and dominated by her. Rudolf Lorenz, a tall and good looking 20 year old, seemed to be the Baroness' favorite. Robert Philippson was much stronger and taller. The Ecuadorian, Valdivieso, a long time inhabitant of Isabella Island who had traveled to France, now formed part of the Baroness' train.

The very first night they slept on "Friedo" was spent listening to the impertinent woman's complaints of imagined pains so as to call attention to herself. It was just the beginning of the problems that would come.

The Baroness began to take complete control of the island and she let the others know it. She took over the Norwegians' abandoned houses and from there the orange grove that the Wittmer's had lent her out of courtesy. She did whatever was in her own best interests.

A couple of days after the arrival of the Baroness, Heinz went down to Post Office Bay to collect a bag of rice that the boat had brought for him. He could barely believe his ears when the Baroness announced that he had to pay an additional 28 sucres. He thought that there must be some mistake, but, as she demanded her payment, she caressed her revolver. Heinz' protests infuriated her even more and she began to insult both the Wittmers and the Ritters. The Doctor was nothing more than a "lowly dentist or worse yet simply a nurse". Heinz replied that he would no longer lend her his garden where she had set up her tent. She thoroughly ignored his threat and continued to stay there whenever she felt like it.

A couple of days later the Norwegian, Kristian Stamp, and the German writer, Franke, arrived on Floreana, the first to spend a few days hunting and the second to take advantage of their quiet of the islands to write. They had no idea of what was awaiting them. The Baroness refused to allow them to sleep in the Norwegians' house because she insisted that, as she owned the island, she could do as she pleased. Nor would she allow them to hunt since all the animals belonged to her.

Two days after he arrived, Stamp, terrified, bleeding, and pursued by Valdivieso, sought help from the Ritters. Franke had disappeared and it was assumed that he was in hiding to save his life. The hunting of two bulls was the cause for their persecution since they had taken something that did not belong to them. Franke appeared at night and the two found a way to s e c r e t l y leave the island.

What were the Baroness' intentions on the Galapagos? In newspaper articles and in a discussion with Heinz, the Baroness talked about her grandiose plans of converting the island into a new Miami. She had plans to build a luxury hotel, "Hacienda El Paraiso", in the middle of the island specifically for American millionaires. Lorenz and Phillipson were her business partners in the deal.

The Baroness' fits of megalomania frightened the German colony, especially Dr. Ritter who had written a letter to the governor of the islands denouncing the Baroness. Unfortunately, in spite of their complaints, nothing was done or could be done. The letter simply turned into a headache for the Ritters as they imagined what the Baroness might do once she found out about it.

THE BARONESS ELOISE WAGNER DE BOSQUET AS A YOUNG WOMAN

THE BARONESS AND PHILLIPSON ON FLOREANA, 1933

The year ended with large storm clouds on the horizon. In spite of everything, two events brightened things considerably in that difficult period, Christmas and the birth of the first island native, Rolf Wittmer.

The Wittmers had worked strenuously to finish their house so their son could be born in a comfortable and finished home. Curiously enough just when a storm was predicted, Rolf was born during the night of the first of January, 1933. This contrasted with his personality which reflected the peace and tranquility of his native island.

Because of post—partum complications, Heinz went for Dr. Ritter who quickly gathered up all the necessities for treating Margarita. The news of Rolf's birth made everyone joyful and united, including the Baroness. During that time, everyone felt happy in the Wittmer's house. "The birth of the child," wrote Dora later, "seemed to create a Christmas atmosphere. All differences and disputes disappeared for a while and in their place affection and good will reigned".

Heinz wanted to pay Dr. Ritter for his services but he refused to accept payment, least of all money, which was meaningless on the island. Finally, he agreed to accept some dried meat for his chickens. At the time, everyone laughed at the thought. No one could imagine that later that one detail would foster suspicions of murder.

The Baroness was more caring in her gifts than they could have imagined: a tin of oatmeal for Margarita and, with a woman's intuition, some outfits brought all the way from Germany for Rolf. She also had a special present for Dora, some flower seeds, which she knew she would adore, for her garden. Judging from these moments, Floreana seemed destined to change into a true paradise of tranquility and peace.

The houses of the three families were at a good distance from each other and all at different elevations on the island. "Friedo" was the closest to Black Beach, even though it was a couple of kilometers on a rough and steep trail. Then came the Baroness' "Hacienda El Paraiso", farther removed and off the road that led to Post Office Bay. Finally, the Wittmers built their house near the caves and fresh water springs. Each family had chosen the site that they liked best and had all the land that they needed, besides being able to hunt and fish freely.

How does one explain then how these families came to live and endure a true hell on earth? Was it the intrigues, the suspicions or a curse? All kinds of things happened and it was inevitable that the Baroness would be blamed.

She had proclaimed herself the empress of the island and had acted as one. Dora's intuition made her suspect that the Baroness' title was just a ridiculous sham, as were her affectations and pretensions towards. Judging by her conduct and attitude the inha - bitants of the island and especially the Ritters, she appeared to be a sex maniac with little respect for dignity or friendship, and they were on the alert to her.

Later comments spoke of all kinds of excesses on the part of the Baroness, such as the organization of a nudist camp in "Hacienda El Paraiso". (The same had been said about the Ritters when they first came to the island.)They also spoke of her shocking fancy to bathe in the only tank of water that was used by everyone on the island, a habit that became unbearable in the drought of 1934, when barely a bucketful of water was collected daily. They also spoke of her perverse tendency to slander everyone on the island, with the purpose of keeping all the families in conflict.

Add to this, the internal conflicts of each family and one can imagine what happened and how it would end. The smallest incident turned into a major conflict. This is what happened the day the Baroness, during a lunch at Dora's house, boasted that she had lived the life of high society in Paris. Suddenly the little donkey brayed and Dora got up to look after it. The interruption to the conversation and Dora's attitude led to this acrid comment, "How happy Dr. Ritter would be if he got as much attention as the little donkey." It was a sign of what was going to happen, a most refined vengeance.

A few days later, the little donkey disappeared and when he returned he had been so ill—treated that he did not look the same. Two days later, he disappeared again, but this time for good. Later, they found out that he had been taken during the night surreptitiously to the Wittmer's garden and as Heinz did not pardon intruders, he shot.

The Baroness' overbearing attitude and the acts which she lowered herself to, made everyone suspicious about her past. Where did the French title Baroness de Bosquet come from, when her accent clearly pointed to her Austrian background. How did she know so much about Parisian style while certain other practices reflected her plebeian origins. Did not her frequent references to her life in the Orient cause them to suspect something even more shady in her past? Ever since she first appeared with her three young men and their strange relationship, it was obvious that the Baroness led a turbid life. When they first arrived on the island, Alfred Rudolf Lorenz was the Baroness' favorite, but in a few short months, the privilege passed to Robert Phillipson and Alfred was treated more cruelly with each passing day. Some others temporarily joined the group: the Ecuadorian Felipe Valdivieso and the Danish friend of Captain Bruun, Knut Arends.

Lorenz's fall from favor and his resentment of the Baroness, helped to clear up some of her mysterious past as he confirmed their worst suspicions about her. One day Lorenz revealed to Margarita that the Baroness had been a spy during the war and afterwards, a dancer in Constantinople. There, after meeting a wealthy Frenchman, she added the Baroness to her name, Eloise Baroness Wagner De Bosquet.

She herself told very different stories to the visitors. She told the Dane Hakon Mielche that she was the daughter of a high Austrian official who was sent to the Middle East as superintendent of the railroad construction in Baghdad. From there, she moved to Syria, not Constantinople, where she met a French Air Force officer who introduced her to French society as the Baroness Bosquet.

About her life in Paris, Lorenz revealed that behind her apparent aristocratic ways were the studied poses of an actress who had learned everything in the movies and nightclubs.

Why then had she left Paris and her supposed triumph only to disappear in the Pacific? Given the Baroness' uncontrollable megalomania it is hard to explain. But in his conversations with Dora, Lorenz seemed to unlock this mystery. The reason was the bankrupcy of a certain shop called "Antoinette" on Daumesnil street in Paris. This had been caused by the Baroness' folly. They had more than likely arrived in the Galapagos as fugitives. But even there she was able to use all the guiles she had learned in Paris. The Baroness' theatrical personality and her fantastic plans for attracting North American millionaires had the desired effect, at least in part. Allan Hancock arrived for the second time in the Galapagos in January, 1933, and his visits became more frequent. In February of the same year, another millionaire arrived, Vincent Astor on his yacht "Nourmahal." The millionaires' generosity produced an open competition among the colonists and in the end increased the tension among the families.

RUDOLF LORENZ ON FLOREANA. 1933

The arrival of a yacht was carefully observed by everyone and caused them all to run toward the beach in hopes of mail and presents. When the Baroness did not get a visit from Astor, she exploded in rage and blamed the Ritters for such an insult and even accused them of taking things that had been left for her.

It is possible that the millionaires' gift giving unconsciously damaged the atmosphere for the couples as they got farther and farther away from their original ideals of living simply and naturally. The presents, more expensive each time, brought them closer and closer to the "civilized" material life that they had supposedly left behind.

The Baroness' writings also had the effect of attracting more curious visitors, and this infuriated both the Ritters and the Wittmers. In March of 1933, the "Manuel J. Cobos", a small boat which was in constant contact with the mainland, arrived. It had brought all kinds of mail from Germany, which made them very happy until they read the headlines of some of the Baroness' articles: "Revolution on an island in the Pacific . . . Woman proclaims herself Empress. Opposing forces have been put in prison. The Baroness takes control of the Galapagos... Dr. Ritter, a one time German dentist, opposed to reign of terror, has been captured and imprisoned..."

Other headlines, such as "Pirate Queen of the Galapagos" or "The Empress of Floreana" emulated Robinson Crusoe and at the same time unloaded her hatred of Dr. Ritter.

The Baroness' letters were a combination of tricks, cynicism, and schizophrenia. In some she asked for help, others were invitations or accusations against her neighbors, and some were clear proposals of marriage.

The desired results materialized: the arrival of the millionaires with their offers of gifts, building materials and technical aid for the construction of the hotel on the Galapagos. The affluence of these visitors satisfied the Baroness' lust for publicity and at the same time, the other colonists also benefited from their visits. None the less, the Ritters and the Wittmers argued that these visits were having a negative effect and were contributing to the erosion of peace that they had sought for so long. They were attracting the attention of the local authorities, especially because of all the rumors of scandalous and licentious living.

In May of 1933, the Governor of the Galapagos turned up accompanied by an interpreter, Knut Arends. The Governor had come to investigate the situation. Complaints about the Baroness were showered on him, but in vain. No one could have predicted that the Baroness would get her way to such an extent that she was invited by the Governor to spend a couple of days on San Cristobal.

One can well imagine the anger everyone must have felt at such an outcome to his visit. Such was the fury that some months later Heinz would say that he was ready to take justice in his own hands in view of the inefficiency of the Ecuadorian authorities.

Such an ending is strange in view of the fact that the governor who was also a major in the army, was known to be spartan and incorruptible. Knut Arends' role as the interpreter also raises suspicions as he was later to join the Baroness' entourage and even became one her favorites. There are certain documents which lead one to believe that Knut Arends at this time could not be trusted.

Knut Arends' return to join the Baroness' retinue coincides with the arrival of many new visitors to the island, some of whom have left us reports on the explosive atmosphere in which the colonists lived.

The Baroness' entourage was now formed by Arends, her hunting companion, Philippson, her "official husband", and by Lorenz, a fallen angel, reduced to a human wreck by the Baroness and Philippson's abuse. There were also some temporary residents attracted by the idyllic life on Hacienda El Paraiso, such as, Trygwe Nuggerud, the German journalist Brockman and his brother, Linde and others.

The Baroness' actions were unpredictable and frequently contradictory. One day out hunting with these men, plus an Ecuadorian soldier, the Baroness tried to kill Linde, a very handsome fellow to whom she was attracted. The firing mechanism failed and Arends was wounded instead. The ensuing investigation concluded that the Baroness was the only possible suspect. Her reaction was, as always, very strange. She devoted herself to caring for and pampering the injured one which was her typical response. After injuring an animal she would typically spend the next couple of days nursing it.

The Baroness assumed a wide variety of roles: libertine, aristocrat, actress, intellectual, martyr, thief, and even though it may seem incredible, religious mystic. She wished to appear as if she were sent by God to purify the earth. She told Dr. Ritter that God had appeared to her in her dreams and told her to move to Floreana. She even cloaked her libertine nature in some vague semi-religious halo as many fanatic sects have done. At times she seemed inspired by the thoughts of Nietzsche, "beyond good and evil."

What impression did the Baroness leave on her visitors? In spite of her gifts as an actress and her wily behavior those who dealt closely with her knew what she was really like. Those who were present on the day of the hunt and the attempted assassination reacted with horror. The Brockman brothers, horrified by what they had seen, tried to find a way off the island as soon as they could.

At the same time her reception of tourists and the millionaires was calculated. On a sign in Post Office she invited all to visit "El Paraiso" as follows:

WHOEVER YOU ARE-FRIENDS!

Two hours from here is the hacienda "El Paraiso". It is a spot where the tired traveller has the happiness to find peace, refreshment and quiet on his way through life.

Life - this small portion of eternity which is bound to a clock, is so short. So let us then be happy-let us be good!.

In "El Paraiso", you have only one name-Friend!
With you we will share the salt of the sea, the vegetables of our garden and the fruit of our trees, the cold
water which runs down our cliffs and the good things
friends have brought us when they passed this way.

We will spend one or two moments of life with
you and give you the happiness and peace that God
planted in our hearts and souls when we left the
restless metropolis and journeyed away to the quiet
of the ages, which has spread its cloak over Galapagos.

(signed BARONESS WAGNER-BOSQUET"

Her reception of the guests was studied; she lay on a divan in
provocative clothes surrounded by her entourage of three attractive men. In spite of all her preparations, however sometimes she
slipped up and they found her in her nightdress or washing her
underwear.

For the Danish world traveler Hakon Mielche who s p e n t
some time on Floreana, the Baroness was ridiculous. "The Baroness", he says, "was small and you couldn't call her a beauty.
Besides her thick lips, she wore a pair of huge glasses and even
though her mouth was quite big it was not big enough to cover
her yellowing buck teeth, which reminded me of Mistinguette's
sarcastic caricatures".

As was to be expected, for the inhabitants of Floreana, the
Baroness emboided all that was evil. In spite of the fact that they
lived at a distance and were isolated from each other, they were
still up to date on the goings-on at the Hacienda El Paraiso.

According to Dora, the arrangement of the bedrooms led one
to believe she had a wild sex life. It would not be surprising if cu-
riosity led one or some to actually witness what went on there
and according to Dora this was the case.

On top of the wild sexual habits of the group, was the systematic destruction of Lorenz after he fell from grace. The humilia-

tions, the punishments, and the daily tasks were intended to destroy him morally and physically. More than once, the Baroness threw boiling soup in his face and when he protested or asked for money to return to Germany, Philippson, who was much stronger and better fed than Lorenz, was called upon to intimidate him. He would show up at Friedo looking a complete wreck after a beating or after wandering around the island for days like a fugitive.

Lorenz finally found refuge at Friedo but he was always fearful of reprisals so he went to the Wittmers who took him in, gave him work in the garden , and a place to sleep on the second floor with their son Harry. In spite of everything, the Baroness was still able to win him back and he returned to his martyr's existence on the hacienda after a while.

Lorenz knew that he wanted to return to Germany. He put up several signs in Post Office and wrote to his brother in Dresden, Germany asking for help. He also wrote to the Baroness's husband in France begging for work and offering to help him get a divorce. Lorenz' problem was money. The Baroness kept it hidden and when he did ask her for money, she responded violently. Once Lorenz chair broke open the chest where she kept her things, and Philippson, with the Baroness' approval, brutally beat him until he was unconscious. When he regained consciousness, he dragged himself to the Ritters and then to the Wittmers, after which he disappeared for a time and slept at Post Office Bay with the hope of getting a boat out of that hell.

The Ritters' situation was not at all pleasant. As mentioned, the Doctor's attitude towards women was inspired by Nietzsche's ideas and Shakespeare's play, "the Taming of the Shrew."

Margarita writes in her diary that the Doctor frequently hit Dora. We cannot say for certain the reasons for this behavior but we can guess that jealousy might have had something to do with it. We know that the Baroness included all men in her group and that at the same time, Dora was still attracted to handsome men and did not hide the fact.

The quarrels had grown between the families. We have seen

how the gifts caused envy and suspicion, something that the visitors themselves noted. Margarita describes her feelings as she walked down to the beach during one of Hancock's visits. Everyone was anxious to get there first. All of the Germans were driven by fear and resentment: the Wittmers against the Ritters, the two Ritters between themselves, and everyone against the Baroness. It was an incredible spectacle for the visitors.

Of the three families, only Margarita, the strongest and most dominating personality, was able to keep her family united. By the end of 1933, the Ritter's relationship was disintegrating and if you look at the details, anything could be expected from them. Dr. Ritter was thinking about separating from Dora, making her return to Germany, and sending for Mila Clark to replace her. Certainly this plan was not to Dora's liking and would also reflect the failure of their experiment. All of this would explain Dora's admitting that Dr. Ritter had been very hard on her the past few months . (Garth).

The Baroness' group was reduced to herself and Philippson as Lorenz lived almost permanently with the Wittmers and Arends was recuperating from his wounds in Guayaquil. At the beginning of 1934 then, the colonists' situation was explosive. By the end of the year, the colonists would either flee or kill each other.

The Mystery of the Baroness. March 1934

The year 1934 promised to be ominous and tragic. Since October and November of the previous year, there was a complete lack of the rain and wind which ordinarily announced the coming of the rainy season which lasted from November to May. The heat only reflected the hell which the Floreana colonists were living.

The mail which came sporadically brought warm words from family and friends but also brought the ridiculous headlines and articles written only to satisfy the Baroness' vanity and hunger for publicity. For the other inhabitants of the island, her claim to being the owner of the island infuriated and worried them because they knew that she would do anything to get what she wanted.

In the first days of January 1934, Allan Hancock arrived in his yacht filled with scientists and musicians. He brought presents for the colonists: false teeth for Dr. Ritter, a stove for the Wittmers, and clothes for Rolf. And for the Baroness, she got her day of glory when she was asked to appear in a movie. Hancock had brought with him Emory Johnson, a professional movie maker from Hollywood. In a theme developed by the Baroness and Philippson he filmed them as pirates. This was published in "The Los Angeles Herald" in November 1933. (1)

In spite of her passion for taking on dramatic personalities, it appears that the Baroness had no acting talent and the experiment had no real purpose other than to feed her vanity; a present only a millionaire can give.

On his return to California, Allan Hancock stopped by Floreana on January 30. At this same time, Hakon Mielche, a Dane traveling around the world, also arrived in his yacht. His impressions of Floreana and the Baroness appear in his book, "Let's See if the World is Round."

A couple of days later, another yacht, the 6.000 ton. Stella Maris once owned by Kaiser Wilhelm II, arrived. It was filled with North American tourists who extended an invitation to all the colonists even though only the Ritters and the Baroness attended. It was a very active evening as everyone wanted to know how the inhabitants really lived. The Baroness kept her distance in spite

(1) The Peruvian couple, Pablo Rolando and Rosa Hernandez, left Lima on the ship, Santa Rosa on their honeymoon. After a few days, their boat sank but they are able to save themselves in a lifeboat with 12 members of the crew. They arrive exhausted on the Galapagos and are taken prisoner by some armed men under the Baroness' orders and are imprisoned for four days. On the fifth day, they are taken to the beach and set adrift in two boats, at the mercy of the currents. Rolando must kill three men who attempt to board the boat with intentions of molesting his young wife. After many vicissitudes, they are picked up by a passing boat.

of all the attention. When they left the boat, they got together again on Hancock's Velero III, where Philippson who had come with the pretext of borrowing some medicine, was waiting for them even though his true purpose was simple to ingratiate himself with Allan and his company. Nuggerud, who had tied his small boat, "Dynamite" to the Velero III had just arrived to take orders from the colonists for new provisions. After the good-bye party everyone saw how the Baroness and Philippson headed off towards the beach. As Nuggerud was coming down from the Wittmer's house, he saw a scene so strange that he thought they must be drunk. It was a moonlit night and this was the last time that Nuggerud saw them alive. Never had so many ships been gathered in front of the beach so when the ships set sail, they felt even more lonely.

The suffocating heat reached 120 degrees F (48 degrees C) and there was not a bit of breeze. The plants were losing their greenness and the birds were dying by the hundreds. The spring barely gave enough water to survive. In spite of everything, the Baroness, with her usual disregard for everyone, continued her abusive habit of bathing in the spring.

And so passed the month of February and March arrived with increasing heat that put everyone in a bad mood. Suddenly, events began to occur without knowing who had started them, who were the real protagonists and who were just covering up. Worse yet, in the accounts left to us it is difficult to ascertain who is telling the whole truth and who is hiding some mystery.

Let us look at the colonists' situation beginning in mid March. Lorenz had broken with the Baroness again and was living almost all the time with the Wittmers even though he left and disappeared frequently. Sometimes, under pressure from the owner, he returned to "El Paraiso", and other times he found refuge at Post Office Bay. The Ritters, who lived a life filled with problems, had also broken with Baroness. Heinz visited the Ritters every week and Margarita rarely.

There were no visitors arriving on the island or at least no one noticed them. It was as if the heat was causing the tourists and friends to withdraw even more. Now let's look at how Margarita and Dora describe the events of March 1934.

Margarita Wittmer's Narration

Monday, March 26 . The Wittmers heard an animated conversation coming from the direction of "El Paraiso". They assumed that they had visitors which struck them as odd because they had not seen any boats.

Tuesday March 27. The next morning the Baroness appeared in the Wittmer's garden asking for Lorenz. Margarita told her that he was working outside with Heinz and Harry. Very excited, she told her that a group of friends had invited her to go on a cruise. "We're going to Tahiti," she told her.'I hope that will be a better place to fulfill my plans. Lorenz is staying behind to take care of my things, until I send word to him to do otherwise.'When Lorenz returned he suspected it was a trick. He waited until after lunch to find out what was happening because he assumed by then the boat would have left.

Dora and Friedrich were very happy at the Baroness' supposed departure because of the water crisis. They did not find out any more. Lorenz did not come to work for two days which made them think that the trip had been an ploy to kidnap him. When he finally reappeared (March 30), he told the Wittmers that the hacienda was deserted and that the donkeys along with the majority of the Baroness and Philippson's belongings had disappeared. On the beach at Post Office Bay, he could only find some footprints with no signs of the two. Margarita ran to tell the Ritters the news. Dora was jubilant at the news and,because of Margarita's visit, prepared some chocolate and other delicacies. Friedrich, unlike his usual self, remained aloof and silent.

Margarita counseled Lorenz to leave the island, "Sell whatever you don't want to take and try to find a way back to Germany as soon as possible." Friedrich also warned him to leave quickly.

After a while, they went to the Hacienda with Lorenz and

Heinz. Ritter was opening trunks and boxes with complete abandon as if the Baroness and Philippson had gone forever. Margarita
reprimanded them saying that they had no right to take the Baroness' belongings at which Lorenz replied that everything had been
bought with his money. Everyone took what they needed and
Heinz took what was left over. Dr. Ritter had an uncommon interest in documenting the events but Lorenz was totally opposed
to that. Margarita objected because there were many things that
had not been proved, including the possibility that the Baroness
might return. Dr. Ritter responded, "She won't return. You have
my word on it". It was true that they had not seen a boat, although
from their house they could only see the boats anchored at
Black Beach but not those at Post Office Bay. "Anyway, they've
left," said Ritter, "they've left forever".

Dora Strauch's Narration

March 19, Monday It was mid-day. The heat was insufferable
and no one could work. There was not a breeze and all was calm.
A long shriek broke the silence. It was like some inhuman shout
of terror. It was hard to tell how far away it was and if it was near
or far. Everything returned to calm and Friedrich went to the door
as if waiting for someone but there were no footsteps or calls.
They did not bother to go out and investigate. They would find
out the next day when Heinz came, but he never showed up.

Two days later Lorenz showed up looking much younger and
peaceful. He was another person. The effects of hate and desperation had disappeared. He still appeared sick but he was in good
spirits and looked like his old self. When asked about the Baroness, he responded that he hadn't seen her. He had been with the
Wittmers for three days and she had not looked for him. He
explained in full detail how he hadn't left the Wittmer's garden for
fear that she would fulfill her threat of killing him which she made
the last time she came to see him. He only told her where to find a
wrench that she was looking for but refused to go with her, even
when she suggested that he come to knead the bread and help with

other things that she knew he enjoyed. Dora said that she found all these details very suspicious. Then he abruptly changed the topic and told her that he had found a donkey with two babies nearby.

March 25. Dora's birthday. Heinz arrived with a letter addressed to "Alec" in which life at "El Paraiso" was described. It also made reference to a book that painted Friedrich and Dora in very negative terms. Another newspaper article also described the Ritters in less than laudatory terms. Dora was sure the author was the Baroness because, among other details, it was signed by "Antoinette, Robert and Lorenz". Antoinette was the name of the shop that the Baroness and Lorenz had had in Paris. Dr. Ritter asked how he had gotten the letter and Heinz said that Lorenz had gotten it at the Hacienda. If this were true then Lorenz had been lying when he said that he hadn't been to the Hacienda recently. During the conversation, Heinz was furious at the Baroness, shouting that he would be forced to take the law into his own hands given the lack of protection on the part of the Ecuadorian authorities. A little while later, Margarita arrived with the news that the Baroness and Philippson had disappeared. Dora took the news very calmly, asking many questions. They agreed that they would go the Hacienda on April I.

April 1. Harry and Lorenz arrived with a donkey for Dora to ride because her leg was bothering her. They had agreed to lunch at the Wittmers before going to the Hacienda. They went by the entrance and in spite of the infernal heat, it appeared happy and inviting "like a smiling mask that hides corruption and terrible crimes and memories".

During lunch, which demonstrated Margarita's fine culinary skills, Dora called attention to a damask table cloth and a tea set that she had seen before at a party at the Baroness' house. Margarita was indignant. The tea set she had bought in Guayaquil and the tablecloth had been a gift from her sister in Germany.

After eating, Friedrich put in writing what he had heard from Lorenz and Margarita. Lorenz protested saying that it was useless but Dr. Ritter insisted that it was necessary to clarify the events and leave everything in writing.

They headed towards the hacienda in spite of their repugnance towards the place. Upon entering, "a sudden, searing wind shook the whole area, scattering the banana leaves as if they were straw". Lorenz led the group, followed by the Wittmers, then Dora and Friedrich. The first thing they noticed was the Baroness' hat which was on the table. In a corner was her suitcase, filled as always. Everything was clean and orderly as was her custom. The photographs, including the picture of her grandmother were still in their places. But most surprising of all was to see the book *The Portrait of Dorian Gray* on the table since the Baroness, who considered it a good luck charm, never parted with it. How could she ever have left it behind on her cruise to Tahiti?

5. A Key Witness Disappears, July 1934.

During the cold of the nordic winter, news travels slowly and it took a while for the outside world to hear of the Baroness' disappearance.

On Floreana, nothing had changed in appearance. In the midst of a heat wave which isolated them even more from the world, the colonists struggled to survive. Rudolf Lorenz continued to live tranquilly with the Wittmers. Margarita observed him closely and later told Waldo Schmitt that while he was with them, he would go off for hours and when asked where he had been, he answered "at the windy spot" alluding to the isolated area where the feral cattle grazed.

On April 21, it finally rained and they heard a boat's whistle. The Wittmer's and Lorenz went down, but the ship continued to Post Office Bay where it anchored. It was the yacht that belonged to the Chicago millionaire Howell. They had come for the Baroness but were given the news that she had disappeared. Lorenz wanted to leave on the yacht to return to Germany but did not have time to pack his things since the yacht was setting sail at midnight.

Howell left a gift of some bags of seed. This brought on new rifts between the families. Margarita would write, "a sad state of affairs, all Germans on the island and all enemies".

In July the rains came and with them the opportunity to plant again. The drought had burned everything.

Lorenz seemed tranquil but without warning he would wander off to Post Office Bay and then back to the Wittmers. They would sometimes find him hiding in a corner, quietly crying.

Around mid July 1934, Trygve Nuggerud arrived in his small fishing boat, "Dinamita", with one sailor, Triviño, and two passengers, young Rolf Blomberg from Sweden and Artur Wörm-Muller, an old friend of Captain Bruun. Nuggerud had just recently married a young Ecuadorian woman with big dark eyes and was soon to be a father. Nuggerud, according to Blomberg, was as happy as a lark at the idea of being a father and didn't know what to do in the months that still lay ahead of him. To kill time, he decided to visit Floreana and leave some coffee plants that he had promised the Baroness. The young explorer Blomberg and Wörm-Muller took advantage of the trip, the former to renew his friendship with Dr. Ritter and the latter to find out if the stories about the Baroness were true.

On the beach at Post Office, they found this sign:

"A jung man in the interior here is forced to leave the island, because he has no longer any more a living here. Therefore he begs every shyp for an ocasion to take him off to Chatham or Guayaquil. I live by caverne, way marked road (red), 1 auer to go.

May 27, 1934   Rudolf Lorenz"

Blomberg, Triviño and Nuggerud followed the trail marked with animal skeletons, a reminder of the Baroness' useless killings, towards "El Paraiso". Worm-Muller remained at Post Office Bay. As they walked through the gardens and fields under cultivation, they saw not a soul. They shouted but heard only their own far-off echo. They returned to the Wittmer's house. The Wittmers, along with Lorenz, ran out to greet them, anxious for mail. Lorenz was thin and sickly looking. After introducing themselves.

TRYGVE NUGGERUD, " happy as a lark" as Blomberg described him.

(Stein Hoff: Drommem om Galapagos, 1985, p. 153.

they asked about the Baroness. The reply was that, "she disappeared". Margarita spoke to them of the Baroness' supposed trip and Lorenz told how they had found the house empty and the footprints on the beach at Post Office.

They spent the night at the Wittmer's house and after visiting the Ritters, returned to their boat guided by Lorenz, who was auxious to leave for Chatham and from there to Guayaquil.

The good-bye between Lorenz and Dora was bitter because she still resented him, while his relationship with the Wittmers was very cordial. The "Dinamita" headed towards Santa Cruz and in route passed the "San Cristobal" which was carrying sulfur from the volcanoes on Isabella to Chatham and Guayaquil. This was Lorenz's opportunity. The two Scandinavians and Triviño stayed on Santa Cruz and the next day, Nuggerud, Lorenz and a boy, José Pazmiño, set sail for Chatham, where they would catch the "San Cristobal" to Guayaquil. From the beach, they watched as Nuggerud, Lorenz and José Pasmiño sailed off into a calm sea. A couple of days later, Blomberg got the news that the "Dinamita" had not arrived on Chatham and no one knew its fate. They along with the ship "San Cristobal" spent several weeks looking for them but with no results. The general opinion was that the boat had sunk and all had drowned. A month later, Blomberg sent the Wittmers a letter, via Post Office, in which he recounted Nuggerud's journey and the fear that he and his companions had all died tragically at sea. Before leaving the Galapagos in route to the mainland, Blomberg visited Nuggerud's young widow. He would never forget the picture of that woman whose "big dark eyes" were filled with tears, while in arms was her young son, a living portrait of Nuggerud.

In the summer months many visitors arrived to see the Baroness and were surprised to hear that she had disappeared and no one seemed to be able to give any explanation. Some Germans, "globetrotters" as Margarita called them, came and tried to live on the island but their enthusiasm was short lived.

Meanwhile, since the Baroness' disappearance, the Ritters' problems had not been resolved and seemed even worse. Separation and Dora's departure were just a matter of time, according to Margarita. On the other hand, Dora's version is totally the opposite.

Margarita's Account

"Dora and Friedrich's situation was deteriorating rapidly and they talked about leaving the island since they hadn't found what they were looking for there. For Dr. Ritter, it was just another disillusion. His fights with Dora got worse and they only waited for Allan Hancock's arrival to take her to the mainland".

Dora Strauch's Account

"Friedrich's personality had changed and he ceased all agricultural tasks in order to dedicate more time to his philosophical studies. He was now in a very creative period. We had found perfect harmony and peace together. All our differences had blurred and we had come to an inexpressible understanding that words can not explain.

Friedrich had become very tender and considerate again. All the storms had ceased. A happiness and stability which we had never known before this month, united us in a more human way".

Phillip Lord of the United States network, NBC, arrived on Floreana on the sailboat "Seth Parker" on November 6, 1936 in search of material for his radio programs. He wanted to speak to the two families that were increasingly antagonistic. While Lord was eating with Wittmers, the sailors arrived from Friedo with the news that all of the Ritter's chickens were dead. It seemed that they were poisoned by meat. Was it the preserved meat that Lord had given them or the meat that Dr. Ritter had accepted in lieu of payment for his services when Rolf was born?

Two days later, according to Margarita, the Wittmers, in spite of the antagonism between the two, took chickens and a rooster to the Ritters to help them begin again. The doctor insisted that the bad meat could be eaten if it were boiled for a long time and he offered them some but they politely refused.

A couple of days later tragedy suddenly occurred.

Margarita Wittmer's Account

Nov. 20 Margarita heard some hurried footsteps heading towards her house. It was Dora who had come limping. She did not take time for greetings but exclaimed, "Something terrible has happened Frau Wittmer. Dr. Ritter has eaten poisoned meat. He's sick and I think he is dying". She entered the house and fell into a chair.

Two days earlier, they had opened up some cans of meat and saw that the meat was spoiled. However he insisted that with a good boiling there would be no danger, so they ate. Dora felt poorly but Friedrich was really sick.

Margarita got a rubber hose for taking the poison out of his stomach, left a note for Heinz and then left as quickly as possible. When they arrived at Friedo, she realized that it was too late to pump his stomach. Friedrich couldn't make himself understood and some of the last intelligible words he uttered were how ironic it was that a vegetarian would die from eating poisoned meat. After that, he was only able to write a few notes, and in spite of the pain, he would not let Dora give him an injection of morphine. At nightfall, with great effort, he was able to write a note which said, "I curse you with my last breath" and he looked at Dora with his eyes filled with hatred. Dora avoided his glance and when she attempted to get near him, he tried to hit and kick her. At night he calmed down, while Margarita took care of him and Dora went off to rest.

At 9 in the morning, sensing that Dora was entering his room, Friedrich, looking like a ghost, sat up. He tried to hit her again. His eyes shone feverously as if lit by a wild flame. Dora gave a cry and ran off horrified. Friedrich fell onto the pillows and died.

Heinz had come over during the night but had returned to see to the children. Margarita accompanied Dora who talked incessantly about different topics and frequently mentioned a secret that Friedrich and Lorenz shared that she could not understand. Margarita had the impression that there were times when Dr. Ritter wanted to ask her forgiveness. Dora also had a premonition for a while that if she did not leave the island she would be killed but she continued to talk about the Doctor's writings and how they would be considered masterpieces one day.

The Doctor died on November 21, 1934. For the funeral, Margarita brought flowers for Dr. Ritter's tomb. Dora did not attend the funeral.

Dora's Account

After the paragraps in which she describes her supposedly harmonious idyll, Dora relates the end. "He woke up sick perhaps from the stroke which left his right side paralyzed. While he remained still, he repeated to me what he had told me so many times before, "I have fulfilled my work on earth. In the material realm, I have built Friedo; in the spiritual world, I have learned to control my emotionss and feelings; and in the world of the mind, I have designed and written my philosophy but work in the religious sphere is the ultimate reality. The fusion of the ego with everything can only be accomplished through death." She then read him his favorite passages from "Thus Spoke Zarathustra".

When he was feeling worse, he asked for his revolver but she refused to give it to him. The Wittmers arrived and they also sat with him through the night. She nodded off and suddenly awoke with a jolt. It was the last convulsions of death. "He opened his blue eyes and extended his hands towards me. It was a calm and happy look and it seemed to say, "I am leaving but promise me that you will not forget our dream."

The next day, Heinz and Harry went to bury the body at Friedo. They wrapped him up in a linen cloth that they had brought from Germany, put him in a small cart and took him to a tomb dug amidst the stones of the garden that he had so laboriously tilled and leveled with his own hands.

A Macabre Finding on Marchena Island November-December 1934

The tragic year of 1934 ended with the impression that anything could happen. The disappearance of the Baroness and Philippson, the loss at sea of Lorenz, Nuggerud and Pazmiño, and the death of Dr. Ritter were all events surrounded by mystery and suspicions. The percentages were shocking. Of the seven people on Floreana, four had disappeared tragically and mysteriously without counting the two from other islands, Pazmiño and Nuggerud.

The mysterious disappearance of "Dinamita" was cleared up by mid November. Lorenz and Nugerrud's bodies were found on Marchena Island on November 17, by a tuna boat, the "Santa Amaro" of California, that was tranquilly fishing in Ecuadorian waters.

Captain William Borthen found them and passed on the news by radio. The complete story appeared in the December 13, 1934 edition of the *New York Times*. It reads as follows:

> It was 4 p.m., Nov. 17. As I swung the Santa Amaro around to anchor off Marchena Island, I glanced ashore and spotted a mast with remnants of cloth at its top. With four crew members, I went ashore and found the bodies, about seventy five feet from the water-line and twenty feet apart.
>
> Near the bodies I found about thirty letters helter skelter. I also found hundreds of burnt matches and a small pile of wood with charred paper beneath it, evidence that the men had failed in their effort to start a fire. Nearby was the carcass of a seal. The men apparently had captured the seal, killed it with a rock, drunk its blood to allay thirst, and then torn the animal apart with bare hands and eaten some of it for food. Several safety razor blades also were found.

Both men undoubtely died of thirst and starvation. Wittmer (i. e. Nuggerud) perhaps died first, and Lorenz covered him with the skiff. Indications were that the men had been dead several months".

Captain Borthen did not find any signs of Jose Pazmiño or of the boat "Dinamita". He left the bodies as he found them, picked up the letters and some of the children's clothing, which was a present from Margarita for her sister which Lorenz had promised to deliver.

The newspaper accounts caused a furor for a time. Hancock's "Velero III" left California the 23 of November. When they heard of Borthen's find, they planned to visit Marchena Island to identify the bodies. There were three biologists on board who would help with the painful task: Waldo Schmitt, Fred Zienenhenne and S. Garth.

The bodies were found. Lorenz weighed only twenty pounds and Garth upon seeing it commented, "I couldn't help but think that I was looking at the Baroness and Philippson's assassin."

How does one explain this tragedy? One can never know for sure but one can imagine. The motor must have failed between Santa Cruz and Chatham and as the boat couldn't hold its own against the strong currents, it was pulled north and ended up on Marchena Island. Maybe they jumped out before the boat sank and perhaps the boat continued on with the boy on board. The small boat without oars next to the two bodies might be from a previous shipwreck. The mystery will never be resolved.

Velero III dropped anchor at Black Beach on December 4. Allan Hancock asked about the inhabitants of the island. Margarita responded, "I fear I have some bad news. Dr. Ritter died three weeks ago. It's been a blow for Miss Dora and I've been taking care of her a little." The Captain told of the tragic deaths of Nuggerud and Lorenz and made reference to Dr. Ritter's letter in which he spoke of the Baroness' disappearance.

THE TRAGEDY OF MARCHENA ISLAN

The mummified bodies of Nuggerud (rear) and Lorenz (foreground).

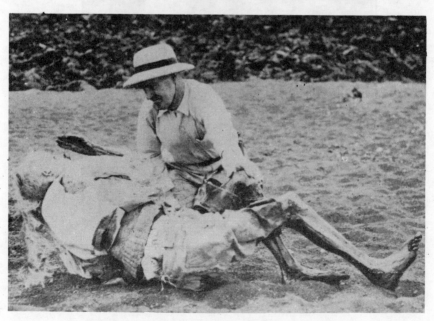

The mommified body of Rudolf Lorenz. December 1934.

(Stein Hoff: Drommen om Galapagos, p. 154)

- 173 -

MARIA RODRIGUEZ, the girl of "big black eyes" with her son on her arms.

In their conversations with the colonists certain facts stood out. John Garth recounts how Dora said that Friedrich "had been very abusive to her in the last few days".

They visited the Baroness' house and found that everything had been demolished. All the news was transmitted by radio but certain details Hancock would not allow to be divulged, especially when he found out that an Ecuadorian journalist from the newspaper, 'El Telegrafo", was hanging around Post Office Bay in search of a story.

Dora took advantage of the presence of the millionaire's yacht to leave Floreana for Germany. On the morning of December 7, Allan arrived at Friedo with some of his companions from the yacht to pick her up. Dora looked thin and tired, but she still had the same spirit that had impressed Hancock. She visited Friedrich's tomb for the last time, posed for a photograph and they all returned to Friedo to pick up her things, Dora burst into tears and Margarita did the same. Heinz and the crew helped to carry her belongings, most of which were nothing other that trash, in innumerable boxes. They boarded the ship at 4:15 on a cloudy December day.

In the following paragraph, Dora describes her good-bye to Floreana.

> "I said good-bye to Friedrich's tomb but I didn't feel as though I were leaving him in Floreana's cold, hostile ground. It was a strange feeling that I can't explain in words but I felt that he wasn't dead but simply without a body. And it was as if a thought, a spiritual enlightenment came over me. I knew that the great work that I had found in him had only just begun. The look on his face when he died told me that our experiment hadn't failed. That Floreana was one stage of our work in life, I am certain. The gods of Floreana killed Friedrich but they don't have any power over him. He will continue living through me".

During the trip, Dora gave increasingly alarming and contradictory information regarding the past events: Friedrich had eaten poisoned chicken in spite of Dora having warmed him not to do it; exasperated, she had decided to kill him and return to Germany; and the Wittmers were involved the Baroness' disappearance, etc.

The last statement made Hancock return to Floreana to clear up the matter. At his insistence, Dora and Margarita signed a joint declaration regarding the main facts of the Baroness' disappearance.

Velero III set sail the 15th of December for Chatham where Dora was interrogated by the Governor. She was accompanied by Waldo Schmitt and John Garth who acted as her interpreters. In her declaration, Dora confirmed that Friedrich died "after having eaten rotten chicken."

Hancock and his companions were anxious to see Dora free to continue her trip to Germany even though they didn't explain why they were so interested. With a sigh of relief, they watched as the Governor signed the death certificate and the permit for Dora to continue on to Guayaquil.

After a quick trip to Española Island they headed to Guayaquil where a whole army of newspaper reporters awaited them. They were able to avoid the majority of them even though some were able to slip through. Dora, under Hancock's orders, did not say a word.

There, they met up with some acquaintances who were returning to the Galapagos; Knut Arends, who had completely recovered from his wound, was among them. Surprisingly enough, they heard him say that he had a wonderful time with the Baroness and that he would gladly return if he had the opportunity.

Dora spent Christmas on Velero III and shortly thereafter the steamer "Cali" left for Germany on the 2nd. of January, 1935. Dora had been protected by Hancock up to this point and what would come later was her responsability.

The Wittmers were left behind to face the authorities, visitors and reporters who were invading the island. The most difficult thing to deal with were the investigations, the first conducted by the Governor of the Islands, who arrived with an interpreter and a reporter named Luna. Through h i m, t h e y learned of Friedrich's suspicions that Margarita was involved in the Baroness and Philippson's disappearance. The Wittmers were able to refute the accusations so well so that the Governor stayed to eat with them.

In the mail from Germany, the Wittmers received all kinds of proposals for their exclusive story about the recent mysteries. Margarita made use of one of these propositions to travel with young Rolf to Germany.

In the German consulate in Guayaquil, she not only had reporters, but a whole court of six people including a judge, awaiting her. The inquiry lasted three hours which tried the patience of little Rolf who exploded in tears because of the tension.

In Cologne, where her family awaited her, Margarita had the opportunity to speak out on the latest events on Floreana. Here, after her statements, war broke out between Dora and Margarita. Dora, who was living in Berlin, embarked on her book, "Satan came to Eden", which was published that same year in German and English.

Margarita's book, which was a collection of her newspaper articles, was prevented from coming to press by the Baroness' brother, who was a high official in the Nazi Party.

Margarita returned to the Galapagos in January, 1936, and found some pleasant changes in her house. In 1937, a new "native of Floreana" was born, Ingeborg-Floreanita. That same year some new colonists arrived, the Zabala family, who settled on Friedo, the Cruz family, and finally the U.S. citizens, Frances and Aislie Conway. The Conways won Margarita's confidence and tried to clear up some of the fuzzier details of the Baroness' disappearance but unsuccessfully. Whenever they asked her anything about it they always got the same reply, "We had so many problems with the Baroness that we don't even like to talk about her."

Then the war came. Baltra Island was occupied by United States military forces and then lent by the Ecuadorian government as their contribution to the war effort. The Conways left Floreana. Frances to work on Baltra and Aislie in California. In spite of their German nationality, the Wittmers were not bothered, but a detachment of Ecuadorian soldiers was established on the island.

In 1951, Harry Wittmer was drowned when his small fishing boat capsized. In 1956, Rolf and Ingeborg Floreanita both married Ecuadorians. From this brother and sister, a third Wittmer generation was born. In the sixties, Floreana once again received world wide attention with the disappearance of two people, an American tourist in 1964 and Mario, Floreanita's husband in 1968. Inquiries followed and rumors once again pointed to Margarita in these disappearances.

In 1980, one of the mysteries was solved when the skeleton of the North American woman was found. She had died from exhaustion and exposure. The mysterious disappearance of Mario has yet to be solved.

Heinz Wittmer died in 1969, having fulfilled Hakon Mielche's prediction. "When all the other colonists have turned to dust, Heinz will still be smoking his pipe in his cozy home and he will have forgotten to count the days."

Dora Strauch died in Berlin in 1942.

Margarita Wittmer still lives in her house in Black Beach with her family and refuses to talk about the events of over 50 years ago.

Could Sherlock Holmes Solve All the Enigmas?

After the events of 1934 and all the facts that we have just laid out were made known to the public, a flurry of speculation ensued without any conclusive results.

Fifty years have gone by and in spite of all the analysis, nothing has been cleared up. Surely, even the famous detective Sherlock Holmes would find himself perplexed and incapable of concluding his study of this case with his usual, "Elementary, my dear Watson."

The facts are relatively simple. Of the seven participants in the tragedy, four disappeared or died mysteriously or tragically, the Baroness, Philippson, Dr. Ritter and Lorenz. The two survivors , Dora and Margarita, left us their accounts, apparently complete, along with the testimony, writings and letters of the other colonists, friends and visitors who were close to the protagonists either before or after the events; such as Hancock, Garth, Blomberg, Wörm-Muller, Hakon Mielche, Waldo Schmitt, and others.

As a whole, there is a large body of information that could be enough for an exhaustive analysis by a detective or historian. Let us not take into account previous popular rumors because the majority are based on subjective opinions ., simple suspicions or personal likes and dislikes. Let us also discount certain comments made abroad which blamed the Ecuadorians for killing Dr. Ritter.

We should start with Margarita and Dora's accounts first because they are the most complete and immediate and second because the other testimonies tend to corroborate or cast doubts on their veracity. The two protagonists write about the same facts and the obvious question is which one of the two should we believe?

Dora Strauch changed her testimony many times and other times she contradicted herself. But, can we conclude that her whole story is false? Margarita's memories are more complete and consistent, but she leaves some strange gaps which lead one to think that she is hiding something. These gaps and ambiguities have harmed her. Some have even painted her as Mephistopheles or a symbol of polished evil, without a doubt, unjustly.

Let's look at the personalities and actions of the main characters.

Rudolf Lorenz

He is without a doubt the principal suspect in the Baroness and Philippson's disappearance as much because of his motives as his behavior and actions before and after the event. His capacity to react and make decisions was very slow but he might have killed them in a burst of jealousy, providing the circumstances were right; such as, if he had a weapon, found them sleeping or drunk, or had a third person helping him.

Dr. Ritter and Margarita appeared certain or at least suspected he was guilty and tried to persuade Lorenz to return to Germany as soon as possible.

When Lorenz reports the Baroness' disappearance, he unconsciously incriminates himself. He states, "The Baroness has disappeared , her donkeys have also disappeared, and there are some footprints at Post Office Bay." This would be equivalent to saying "the Baroness and Philippson's bodies were transferred on donkeys to the environs of Post Office Bay." Everyone knows that the area is infested with sharks.

In defence of Lorenz is the disappearance of the Baroness' money. If he had been the killer, he would have taken the most valuable things for himself, but before and after his death nothing was found unless the valuables were lost when Nuggerud's boat went down.

Dr. Friedrich Ritter

Dr. Ritter had a violent nature and had reasons for killing the Baroness. If Lorenz had any accomplices, he would be the most likely suspect. After the Baroness' disappearance, Ritter's actions and words lead one to suspect that he had something to do with it. He was afraid that "a bullet might come from the thicket even though the Baroness is no longer here." Why did he have this fear?

Dr. Ritter, according to Margarita's account, was extremely pleased when he heard of the Baroness' disappearance and, when at the Hacienda "El Paraiso", seemed fairly certain that the Baroness would not return.

Dr. Ritter frequently changed his version of the story which perhaps indicates that he was trying to cover up something. In a letter found next to Lorenz' body, he writes, "The Baroness and Philippson have disappeared in the South Seas". In another version, in his statements published in a Guayaquil newspaper, he states that he heard a woman's shout and a shot fired. He suggested to Blomberg that the Baroness and Philippson had committed suicide.

Margarita Wittmer

Margarita was a resilient and domineering woman who seemed to be the principle motivator in the family. She was a practical and ambitious woman. She had many reasons to kill the Baroness for whom she felt a strong dislike. The antagonism between the two women was almost a declared war. The fact that she was Lorenz's confidant, makes her a suspect of either collaboration or cover up.

Margarita was the only one who spoke of a boat that was ready to take the Baroness to the South Pacific. For many, including the Conways, the appearance of a boat that no one saw or found out about is curious, given that in similar circumstances, everyone ran down to the beach immediately. It seemed to be a clumsy invention. It is possible that it was made up by the Baroness to entrap Lorenz and was taken as fact by Margarita but that is difficult to believe. Some see Margarita behind all the events because, in the end, she took advantage of the circumstances.

In defense of Margarita, one must look at her consistent attitude in all inquiries, on the island, in San Cristobal and in Guayaquil. She confronted everyone without help or protection from anyone. In Margarita's and Dora's joint statement of December 15th, 1934, which would be the equivalent of a match, Margarita sticks to her first account, while Dora changes and changes her version until she finally accepts Margarita's account. In her story of Dr. Ritter's death and the poisoning, Margarita is much more consistent and logical than Dora.

Dora Strauch

Dora was not a very stable person. She often made different and contradictory statements regarding the Baroness' disappearance, Dr. Ritter's death, and her deteriorating relationship with him. The following are some specific cases of these inconsistencies: the date of the Baroness' disappearance ; the story of the loud shouting that was at too great a distance to be heard; the accusation against Margarita and the later retraction of it; the idyllic description of the last days and death of Dr. Ritter that do not concur with the confidential information provided by the crew members of Hancock' Velero III and other visitors who spoke of the verbal abuse she received from the Doctor in his last days.

No one believes that Dora directly participated in the Baroness' disappearance but it is likely that she may have known of the circumstances surrounding it. Can we then accuse her of covering up? When refering to Lorenz, Dora said, "a man with blood on his hands" which would imply that she knew he was guilty.

In the middle of the investigations, Dora tried to blame the Wittmers for the Baroness' disappearance. Was this done out of hate or did she know something?

Given Dora's personality, the poisoning of Dr. Ritter cannot be considered a premeditated crime but rather a momentary flight of rage.

Allan Hancock's zeal to protect Dora in the inquiries makes one think that she might reveal something that she shouldn't.

Heinz Wittmer

His personality in this whole drama is very unclear and he has never been considered a suspect in any crime. He was capable of anger as seen when he stated that he would "take the law into his own hands if the Ecuadorian authorities continued to ignore the problems" but no one took him seriously.

Could he have been involved in a cover-up? If Margarita was Lorenz' confidant it is difficult to believe that he did not know the facts of the matter.

Given these factors, let us try and shed some light on the mystery and pose some possible theories and hypotheses. In the first place let us look at the obvious questions and answers which will help clear up some of the problems.

First Question

Did or did not a boat arrive that was going to take the Baroness to the South Pacific? If it did arrive, then why didn't anyone disembark as was usually the case? If it didn't arrive, who made up the story and why?

Second Question

What was Lorenz doing during the two days he was absent from the Wittmer's house, after he found out that the Baroness was looking for him?

Third Question

What happened to the Baroness' money? Lorenz didn't take it or at least it wasn't found in his possession.

Fourth Question

How does one explain Dr. Ritter's fear that a bullet would be fired from the undergrowth?

How did the Baroness disappear?

Final Hypotheses in search of a clue to find the solution.

Hypothesis I (a la Sherlock Holmes)

1.— The·Baroness and Phillipson arrive at the Wittmer's house to pick up Lorenz but he has already gone off with Heinz. They probably do not mention the presence of the boat.

2.— Lorenz upon returning finds out that they were looking for him and suspects a trap. He then disappears for two days!

3.— Lorenz manages to kill the Baroness and Philippson on the 27 or 28 of March, 1934, but by what means, we will never know. He probably takes advantage of favorable circumstances or follows a premeditated plan.

4.— His accomplice, if he had any, was Dr. Ritter.

5.— The Baroness and Philippson's bodies disappear in some unknown spot, probably close to Post Office Bay where sharks are plentiful. That would explain the disappearance of the donkeys from the Hacienda "El Paraiso" and the footprints that Lorenz mentioned.

6.— Margarita hears of the Baroness' assassination from Lorenz and tries to protect him. She makes up the story of the boat and the cruise to the South Pacific. Dora is told of the Baroness' murder by Lorenz and suspects Dr. Ritter's participation in the crime.

7.— Dr. Ritter and Margarita insist that Lorenz return to Germany as soon as possible. They fear that Lorenz might shoot Ritter from the bushes just as he killed the Baroness or that during the investigation, he might implicate Dr. Ritter in the crime.

Hypothesis II (a la Cruz)

1.— Lorenz kills them both with the knowledge and consent of Margarita, who has been his confidant over the last few months.

2.– Margarita tries to conceal the crime by making up the story of the nearby boat which is cruising to the Pacific, a "clumsy invention."

3.– Margarita benefits from the disappearance. Dora notices that the table cloth and tableware that Margarita is now using belonged to the Baroness.

4.– The Ritters suspect Margarita's involvement in the crime and accuse her although without any convincing evidence.

5.– Lorenz lives at the Wittmer's expense while he is waiting for a boat to return to Germany. The Ritters fear reprisals, perhaps a shot from the undergrowth!

6.– Allan Hancock convinces the two women, Margarita and Dora, to agree on a statement that doesn't implicate anyone. In exchange, Hancock protects Dora in the subsequent investigations, where suspicious aspects of her story might be uncovered, and helps her return to Germany.

Which of the two hypotheses has more aspects of truth?

Undoubtedly, the first hypothesis is based on facts more likely to have happened while the second has many subjective interpretations, all of which revolve around Margarita Wittmer as the prime mover behind the evil deeds which occurred on Floreana. In any case, Margarita Wittmer, as the last living protagonist of this drama, is at the least suspected of concealing information essential to solving this enigma. She and only she, as long as she lives, can shed light on the mystery. On the contrary, it will remain forever the Enigma of Floreana.

Additional Readings

Blomberg, Rolf. **The Galapagos Islands.** Stockholm, 1952.
Conway, Ainslie and Frances. **The Enchanted Islands.** London, 1948.
Strauch, Dora. **Satan Came to Eden.** London, 1935.
Treherne, John. **The Galapagos Affair.** London, 1983.
Wittmer, Margaret, **Floreana.** London, 1961.

ISLA ISABELA (ALBEMARLE)

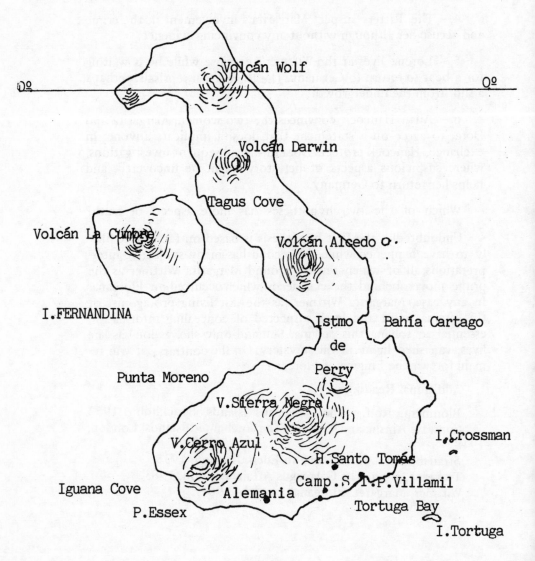

Roca Redonda

Volcán Wolf

0°   0°

Volcán Darwin

Tagus Cove

Volcán La Cumbre

Volcán Alcedo

I.FERNANDINA

Istmo
de
Perry

Bahía Cartago

Punta Moreno

V.Sierra Negra

V.Cerro Azul

I.Crossman

H.Santo Tomás

Iguana Cove

Camp.S.T.P.Villamil

Alemania

Tortuga Bay

P.Essex

I.Tortuga

CHAPTER X

ALBEMARLE: THE HORRORS OF A PENAL COLONY
(1946 – 1959)

A young Ecuadorian Navy Officer carefully guided his ship between the small islands of Crossman and Brattle on route to Puerto Villamil at the southern end of Albemarle (Isabela) Island. He had visited these seas before, but this was the first time he had commanded that ship through such difficult waters, full of submerged lava rocks which appeared everywhere. Concentrating on these maneuvers he had forgotten what had filled his mind during the trip from Puerto Baquerizo, capital of the Archipelago and headquarters of the Chatham (San Cristobal) District Naval Base. As the newly—named commander of the District, he had to visit the Albemarle Penal Colony once a month to leave supplies. He had heard all kinds of rumors, many of them contradictory, but this only increased the expectation of having to visit the colony personally and see the reality of that dread corner of his jurisdiction.

The last outcrops of lava appeared, some of them covered with green mangrove, and then the coast with its small volcanic cones and the town of Villamil. After skillful maneuvering, he headed the boat towards the port, slowed down, lowered the anchor and a few minutes later stopped a short distance from the beach.

While the crew was preparing to unload the numerous crates of supplies, the officer went ahead to the beach where the policemen were already lined up waiting him, and farther off, almost a hundred untidy prisoners stood. After the typical military salute, the Chief of the Police Post, reported briefly:

"Commander, nothing to report, thirty prisoners fewer". Many years later he still recalled the impact of such a cold report.

The crew continued to pile the crates on the dock, but the commander's attention was concentrated on the report of the Chief of the Post. There were three camps for the prisoners: Puerto

Villamil for innofensive prisoners or those who had almost completed their sentence; Santo Tomás about 6 kilometers from the town, and "Alemania" farthest away was at a distance of 45 kilometers.

The last crate fell heavily on the ground and the sweaty sailors stepped back a few meters. The ship's crew had finished their job; now it was up to the Colony. The policemen called the prisoners to attention and the column moved towards the crates. Panting from the effort, each of the prisoners threw one of the heavy boxes or sacks onto his shoulders: a hundredweight of rice, a hundredweight of sugar, a crate of noodles ... They turned laboriously and went away down the dusty path until they disappeared from sight on the road to Santo Tomás. There were almost a hundred of them. The crates were all gone, but there were still about thirty prisoners leaving the port. "They're the replacements" — said the policeman — "some of them collapse along the road, so we bring an extra group for those cases".

— "And what do you do with those that collapse?, asked the Navy officer.

— "We bury them when we can, and if not ....."

As his imagination formed a dantesque picture about that "if not ..." the officer returned to the ship. Happily, on future voyages, he would realize that not all of the police reports were so lugubrious as the first one and that the gloomy reality of the penal colony also had its rays of sunshine and human characteristics that built up hope.

The caravan of the prisoners headed for the Camp of Santo Tomás, the first stage of a long trip that would end at "Nueva Alemania", the next day. The Santo Tomas Camp was located in an ancient, extinct crater and occupied the instalations of a North American military base, left from the Second World War. It was a desolate site, where the worst punishment was the monotonous environment that could produce claustrophobia and desperation in anyone. The land, the forests and the horizon were a gray color that changed little, even in the rainy season. There was not a single drop of water nearby and the prisoners' constant occupation was carrying that precious liquid in hated tin jerry cans, from the town of Villamil along a sandy road under a broiling sun.

The penal camp was set up in 1946 when the North American soldiers retreated to Baltra. The instalations were not good for anything except a penal colony. This coincided with the tendency of the authorities on the mainland to send criminals to the most isolated and distant place possible. They could not find a better place than Albemarle.

The arrival of supplies at the Camp occupied all the inhabitants. The heavy bundles were dropped amid sighs of relief, while those in charge of the warehouses took over in their different areas. When evening fell and after a frugal meal, the prisoners were shut up in large barracks and each one lay down on a hard board cot that creaked with every movement, and blended in with the moaning of those who were ill. Their minds hardly funtioned because of their state of exhaustion and a heavy sleep immobilized their bodies.

The "guests" from the Nueva Alemania Camp were accomodated wherever space could be found and spent the night under the surveillance of a policeman. With the sparrows' song before dawn, the guards and prisoners prepared for the long march towards the remote camp before the sun rose. With the shouts and orders, the prisoners took up their loads and disappeared along the narrow path of lava that passed between forests of scalesia. On normal days, they would arrive in a few hours, but with the loads on their backs, that march lasted until evening. Tormented by thirst under the hot sun, some of them collapsed and were immediately replaced by others.

"What do you do with those who collapse? the Naval Officer had asked.

"We bury them there when we can" — the policeman had responded, and if not ..." If they had any strength left to continue, they would arrive at night or the following day and if not the wild dogs would notice their inert bodies.

In a fog from fatigue and thirst, the police and the prisoners arrived at the camp in the evening using their last reserves of energy. They desperately drank jugs of water and at night fell into a heavy sleep. Their only consolation was that they would not have to repeat the trip until the next month.

The "Alemania Camp" was located inside an ancient crater in the mountains on the southern portion of the island. It had more water and arable land, which made it easier to set up farms and orchards for the nourishment of the prisoners.

At first it was a project thought up by a Prison Camp Director who was looking for rehabilitation of the prisoners through work and individual initiative. They received lots of land and the crops were used to improve their situation and accumulate savings to have at the end of their sentences. Some people who saw the project testify that it was a relative success. Several improvised farmers took advantage of the opportunity and worked eagerly. On weekends, they were seen going into town to sell their products and build up savings to begin a new life. Several of those prisoners decided to remain on the island when their sentences had ended and they still live there. Others rejoined society on the mainland.

Unfortunately the experiment was not continued because some of the Colony Directors who arrived later believed only in discipline and punishment and not in "works of charity" as they called those programs. The Nueva Alemania Camp was changed from the experimental farm to a compound for the most dangerous criminals, although the initiative of some policemen helped to improve this image. As time passed, an infirmary for the sick ironically called "El Porvenir" (the future) was built near the sea a short distance from the Port. Here, those who were ill, generally with incurable or contagious diseases such as tuberculosis and syphilis, were shut up. The scarcity of medicine and almost total absence of doctors and nurses, converted this place into a waiting room for death. The bodies of those unfortunate people were buried in abandoned graves which have long ago been forgotten.

Life in the Camp

It is difficult to imagine life in the camp if one has not seen it first hand. It was a mixture of a military camp and a school for boredom. The activities began very early in the morning to take advantage of daylight since electricity, when they had it, was only turned on at night. After a quick breakfast, the prisoners first washed and cleaned up the camp and then they went to work, in the fields in Nueva Alemania and carrying water in Santo Tomas. They worked until sundown, with a lengthy break at midday for lunch.

The amount of work or boredom depended on the capactity and initiative of the directors and the police. A creative director could transform a camp, as occurred in Nueva Alemania; but one with no ideas could make it a hell.

Santo Tomás was the most difficult camp to liven up because of the conditions that have already been described, so the prisoners as well as the police ended up with a dreary and boring life. One of the directors had the idea of building a wall of lava blocks to divide the plain from the extinct crater. With the passage of time, reasons have been invented to explain the construction of a wall inside the camp. The only historical reason was that of forming a barrier to make the prisoners' escape more difficult.

The plan was put into effect with no engineering or studies because they were not thought necessary: a wall did not have mathematical complications, so, in the nerve-racking heat, not thinking about the absurdity of the project and with a slowness inspired by the tortoises, the prisoners began to accumulate blocks of lava in the form of bricks. Then they began to build the first

The Wall of Tears in Santo Tomas Camp (Isabela) buit by the prisioners.

wall ,straight and vertical, without mortar, to a height of ten meters. Since such a weak column could fall down, new adjoining walls held up the first one. Finally the wall ended up curiously rounded at the lower part and weak in the upper part, a portion of which has since fallen. But one could suppose it to be the work of the prisoners themselves in order to prepare an easy way fo escape while the guards were sleeping. Some people say that thirty prisoners died during the construction of the wall. Anything was possible although documentation to confirm this has not been found.

Forty years later, when the island became a tourist attraction, the guides made an effort to invent a story for the visitors to give a reason for something that was done for no reason and was con - cluded thanks only to the power of the whip and the gun.

Many foreign tourists will continue to ask "Why" and "What for", but those who knew that world will feel impatient to see anyone try to find reasons for something that had no reason to exist. The popular imagination has rebaptized this work as the "WALL OF TEARS", in allusion to that of Jerusalem and in memory of the tears of blood of all those who built it, although no one shed a single tear for them. It seems equally ironic to try to stop the prisoners from leaving that suffocating volcano to go to a hamlet of only fifty inhabitants, but which had become a symbol of liberty.

Police vs. prisoners

The Penal Colony of Albemarle was under the direction of the National Police,who used to send personnel there who were judged to be disciplined, harsh and physically strong, to watch over prisoners who had the reputation of being dangerous and incorregible.

The isolation of the island, the few comforts it offered, and the prospect of working with such dangerous people did not make many policemen enthusiastic about going there, in spite of the special bonuses that they received. For these same reasons, for the police, being sent to the Penal Colony was considered an exile.

The criteria for selecting the prisoners were not homogenous. During certain periods, the most dangerous criminals were sent there or even those who could be secretly killed. At other times, groups of newly sentenced prisoners for whom there was no room in the prisons on the mainland were sent there. This allowed them to be divided into the three camps according to how dangerous they were or how long they were staying.

The diversity of the prisoners made it difficult to provide a general solution. There were distinct periods, some of positive work in a pacific environment and others of real oppression with hatred and reprisals between the police and the prisoners.

We have mentioned the case of Nueva Alemania which was converted into a farm, where work and comprehension helped to rehabilitate various individuals, as did the innocuous presence of the prisoners in Villamil. Unfortunately, the preparation of the police at that time was inadequate and they brought with them attitudes and prejudices that increased the problems. In this sense, the police have progressed greatly in recent decades.

There was a widely spread idea that the penal colony was a "university of crime" and far from rehabilitating the prisoners, it made them hardened and daring. For these reasons, the penal colony was the place to take revenge and defend society from bad and dangerous elements. The guards applied iron—handed discipline which was only a step away from eliminating those considered undesirable. Logically, when this type of police dominated, all kinds of abuses and arbitrariness could be expected.

The old chaplain of the Colony recalls several times when he was called to attend to dying prisoners who had been victims of brutal police repression. In some cases, he was only called to certify their deaths. In such an environment, one could expect situations and tragic results that many people still remember.

One of those occurred in 1950, when some police were forcing the prisoners to work like slaves. One day the policeman, Oliverio Camino, ordered a prisoner to clean up the patios and arrange everything for a volleyball game between the guards. He obeyed, but in an unpleasant manner. When Oliverio, standing near him, bet over to tie his shoes, the prisoner leapt on him and stabbed him in the back with a knife. After that, the prisoner fled, but a shot was fired and he fell, dying before his victim. The policeman was given a wake and buried with dignity, while the criminal was placed in a gunny sack and carried to the bottom of a volcano, the site designated for the prisoners, by his companions.

Until a few years ago, the crosses from the massive killings carried out by the police could be seen in this cemetery, which amost no one remembers. The most undesirable prisoners were taken there and the last work done by their hands was digging a ditch, which would become their grave.

"Nothing new", the policeman had greeted the Naval Officer, "thirty prisoners fewer". Perhaps some day, a curious anthropologist will be able to substantiate these massacres, although the names of those who were eliminated will never be known.

In any event, reprisals tended to occur when the prisoners attempted uprisings or mass escapes. That is what happened in 1950 when the prisoners at the Nueva Alemania Camp plotted a rebellion. It was to begin by taking over the camps, killing the police and attacking Puerto Villamil, where they could embark in fishing boats or the boats of a chance tourist in order to return to the mainland.

One of those who knew of the conspiracy was serving a sentence for robbery and did not want to complicate his future with the murders, especially since he only had a short time left to serve. So he denounced the plan to the Camp Director, exaggerating it to be believed. The group of police who had already become known for their harshness, and had, in part, provoked the conspiracy, decided to eliminate the conspirators by blood and fire. Two armed guards presented themselves at the prisoner's cabin the following night and called the first three. Accustomed to these unexpected punishments, they got up grumbling, picked up the water cans to go to carry water as was the custom. They followed the police towards the distant fields. When they were quite far away, the police turned around and began to fire at those unfortunate men. After that, they picked up the water containers and left the bodies for the wild dogs. When the other conspirators realized that they had been betrayed, they ran away to the hills. The police followed them with the intention of killing them, but they did not dare to go too far into that area for fear that they could be ambushed. The prisoners remained there for several months, eating wild fruit, turtle meat and drinking rain water, although some nights they dared to come near the camp where their companions secretly passed them food.

Some months later, the police were changed. The new contingent came with good intentions of helping the prisoners.

Through one who had returned to ask for forgiveness, they let the others know that there would be no reprisals. Tired of wandering through the hills, they surrendered except for two, a homosexual couple who remained at liberty for almost two years.

Attempted escapes were constant and natural, although impossible because of the distance to the mainland. More than once, the escapees ended up lost at sea. The following is what happened one of the few times escaped prisoners reach the mainland.

The fishermen of Villamil usually went out fishing along the southern and western coasts of Albemarle and, after their daily work, they found shelter on the beaches or in small bays to spend the night. Some of the prisoners had observed them and planned an escape. While the fishermen were sleeping, they took over the boats and set out to sea. The shouts of the boats' owners were too late and when they saw that it was hopeless, the fishermen had to return to Villamil amidst incredible suffering.

The fugitives went around the island and headed for the mainland in a suicidal attempt to gain freedom. They intended to row more than a thousand kilometers. When they were in desperate straits from lack of food and water, they were picked up by a boat that took them to Panama. From there they were sent back to Guayaquil when it was discovered that they had escaped from the Galapagos. In spite of everything, as they sailed in the Gulf of Guayaquil near Puná Island, the prisoners jumped ship and hid in the mongrove swamps to the surprise of the captain and guards. In the end, they were captured in the ensuing months and sent back to Galapagos. It is easy to imagine their former companions' surprise when they returned after two years' absence. They thought the escaped prisoners had died at sea.

The memory of that adventure was not pleasant, but a shortening of their suffering was worth it. Luckily, there was not much time left to complete their sentences and they remained on good behavior, recounting their bitter experience to everyone who could listen.

In such a difficult environment, one could expect violence and abnormal situations, especially sexual ones.

Homosexuality was frequent. We have already mentioned the case of the two prisoners who stayed to live as a couple for two years after the mass escape. They had their crops and even made liquor for their parties. On one ocassion they had an argument and one of them returned and informed on the other.

Abnormal cases of sadism were also frequent and attracted more attention due to the danger they entailed.

Those who knew the colony well remember two cases worthy of study; that of the Colombian, Ospina Navia and that of another prisoner, known only by the nickname of "Sastre" (Tailor).

Ospina Navia was the nephew of a former president of Colombia who had the same last name. While he was studying at the University of Quito, for some unknown reason, he associated with the famous thief known as "Aguila Quiteña" (Quito Eagle) in the year of 1949. In an assault on the Cisneros Jewelry store in the capital, the Colombian killed a policeman. A few days later, they were captured in Ambato and sent to the Galapagos Islands. Ospina Navia received a 16 years sentence and his situation was complicated by the attitude of the guards who wanted to get revenge for the death of their comrade.

The psychological state of Ospina rapidly deteriorated and he had a morbid tendency to watch blood flowing. From time to time he was seen capturing an animal, a dog or a burro; he would tie it or hang and discharge his fury, stabbing it with his knife until he felt satisfied and tranquil for some time. His companions at the Camp avoided him, because they never knew when he might act against them.

"Sastre" (Tailor) had been sentenced to 16 years in the Galapagos for the murder of his wife and his nephew in horryfying circumstances. It seems that he also had temporary crises in which he needed to see blood flow in order to calm himself.

The sadistic manifestations of other prisoners were directed against weak or sickly companions whom they tormented just to see them suffer.

Luckily, not everything was gloomy in the Colony and there were also jocose cases, such as that of the "Aguila Quiteña" the thief named Paz, who became famous in the decade of the 40's. He arrived in the Galapagos in 1950 after the assault on the Cisneros Jewelry Store with the Colombian, Ospina Navia, as we have already described. His cleverness had won him the nickname of "Eagle" and he had a very lively intelligence. In the Colony he quickly won the affection of the directors and guards whom he was able to manage as he desired, especially with chess and poker at which he excelled. More than once, he put the police in a bind, taking all their money and even more. On one occasion, a guard lost his clothes and even his official gun, with the ensuing complications.

On the other hand, when he wanted some privileges, he would allow them to win, paying his debts with money received from a not so decent business administered by his lover in Quito. (1) When this woman left him for another man, he no longer received money, but even then his resources for having a good time did not run out.

Somehow he devised a way to send an anonymous letter to the newspapers in Quito and Guayaquil which gave a cry of alarm about the supposedly calamitous situation of the famous "Aguila" and even of his imminent death. Since he was so well known, they were beseiged by commentaries and protest. The authorities secretly gave the Navy orders that they should give a monthly report on the health and general condition of the prisoner. For their part, the directors and guards had heard about the commentaries and rumors that were going around and they were careful to keep him in the best possible condition, especially when the monthly visit of the Chief of the Galapagos Naval District came near. The Aguila Quiteña had achieved what he wanted.

When he completed his sentence for robbery, he returned to the mainland, but since he was very well known, he preferred to settle in Lima, Peru. He died there some time later.

The desire for freedom

The desolation of the colony drove the men to dream of seeking freedom at any cost. They always failed because of the difficulties of overpowering the police and of the distance from the mainland. To solve the first problem, they needed a leader who could organize

(1) This was the "Happy Land" Cabaret in the Northern section of Quito. Under the dance floor they found the jewels that were stolen from the Cisneros Jewelry Store. (Personal information from Mr. Cisneros, owner of the Jewelry Store, August, 1989).

them and solve the practical problems of fleeing. We have already considered some attempts, but the only successful one took place in 1958, because of the presence of a prisoner named Cedeño. He was very intelligent, but, above all, he was an extraordinary leader capable of directing the insurrection.

His nickname was "PATECUCO" and that is what we will call him here.

The 1958 Uprising

The uprising and escape of the prisoners in Febraury, 1958 was the end of an era and of the Penal Colony on Albemarle. Several circumstances contributed to the success of the uprising: the presence of an extraordinary leader, "Patecuco", but also the customary carelessness of the police. The directors lived comfortably in Villamil and did not bother to visit the camps except when it was absolutely necessary, generally at the beginning and end of their tour of duty in the Colony. The camps were under the command of a sergeant (Santo Tomas) and a private first class (Nueva Alemania). The latter had a very high opinion of himself, but was a confirmed drunkard.

Lieutenant Martinez, the new director of the Colony had arrived a few months earlier. He was very young and inexperienced for such a difficult job, which had generally been held by a captain or a major. Discipline had plummeted noticeably. The necessary surveillance was not maintained and prisoners frequently went from one camp to the other.

In this environment it was easy to hatch a plot, which was directed from Nueva Alemania, the farthest camp. It was precisely there that the discipline was most lax and the private first class in charge was frequetly drunk. He was only worried about looking good in front of his superiors.

In January 1958, Patecuco proposed to the director of the Colony that some cultural events be held at the celebration of

February 12, the holiday of the Archipelago. He planned a theatrical evening that would also serve to raise money for the Colony. This would be the second presentation, and it would be better than the first, which had been considered a success. He had written a short farce with the theme of a frustrated rebellion and escape from prison. The piece was so well—written that the private first class himself, wanted to take part as an actor. According to him, the evening was going to be a night of glory, a demonstration of how to manage a penal colony, where so many had failed. Patecuco and those involved in the plot inflated his vanity and proclaimed him the greatest policemen in the world. The private first class sent two prisoners to town to buy demijohns of liquor to "warm up" the rehearsals.

Patecuco and the others had studied the situation well: an alcoholic private first class in Alemania; a vain, careless sergeant in Santo Tomas and a weak, comfort—loving lieutenant in Puerto Villamil. The plan was logical and simple: take over the Alemania camp, immobilize the police and the prisoners who did not adhere to the plan, continue to Santo Tomas and then take Villamil by surprise. From there they could escape in the fishing boats from the port or in some larger boat that they could board on route. Those involved in the conspiracy had obtained enough weapons to begin the uprising. Patecuco was short, dark skinned and had an athletic constitution. He had a penetrating glance and well—defined personality; he was sure of himself, intelligent and made decisions quickly. He had been sent to the Galapagos for robbery, but he had good qualities as he showed on this ocassion.

On the afternoon of February 9, all of the conspirators gathered to go over the last details. Patecuco gave them their last instructions and passed out a shot of liquor, enough to steady their nerves. The guards were drinking and talking unworriedly in a room when Patecuco came in armed with a rifle. "Nobody move this is not an act. It's for real" he shouted.

Before the guards had overcome their astonishment, they were tied up in their chairs and beds.

A generalized shout went around the camp, "We're free" !!

Those who had not adhered to the act were tied up to avoid surprises. The only one missing was "Negro Arevalo" who had gone out hunting and hadn't returned. They went out to look for him, but when he saw them coming, he hid in the undergrowth. He did not want to get involved when he had so little time left before he would be free. In any case, Negro Arevalo, in order to avoid later reprisals and true to his own loyalties did not notify the authorities in the Port.

The attack on Santo Tomas Camp was faster and easier. They arrived at sundown and surrounded it to attack at the best moment. The sergeant who was in charge no longer took the necessary precautions; there were no guards on duty, because he was confident that his capacity was sufficient to dominate any situation. The camp fell without firing a single shot.

The police and prisoners who did not agree to take part in the escape were tied up. The rebels rested for the night, except Pate-cuco, who was attending to last minute details of the attack o n the beach.

The prestige of the conspiracy's leader was at its zenith since everything had turned out as planned. However it could easily have failed if Negro Arevalo or two prisoners who had managed to free themselves had given a warning in the port. The latter, warned the nearby families so that they could flee. Some of them did, but others stayed and fell into hands of seven criminals who went wild that very night.

The attack on Puerto Villamil. February 10, 1958

The beach or the port was somewhat isolated and was the home of the authorities, some merchants such as Mr. Cisneros and the group of prisoners who were considered harmless.

Patecuco gathered the conspirators together very early in the morning and presented them the plan for the day. It had to be obeyed in every detail; personal initiatives were not allowed. In case anything unexpected occurred, he would be replaced by the prisoner nicknamed "Perra Negra" (Black Dog), a black man from Esmeraldas province who was feared by everyone. He was tall and strong and had the appearance of a killer, but inside he was servile, insecure and easy to manage.

The tasks had to be carried out with mathematical accuracy and simultaneously since they were heading for strategic points: three men would neutralize the only radio which belonged to the Navy; four were chosen to attack lieutenant Martinez's house; two men would take over the exercise courts of the prisoners; and the rest would enter the town from different directions when they heard the agreed upon signal.

Day dawned on the beach and life in the port went about its everyday routine: the prisoners were engaged in their jobs and had been working for several hours. The policemen were getting ready for a volley—ball game as they did every day. It was nine o'clock in the morning. Lieutenant Martinez was staying in bed as a result of a sprain he had suffered in the game the day before.

Accustomed to seeing the prisoners walking freely through the streets, no one paid attention to the new arrivals who were setting themselves up in strategic places with weapons hidden under their shirts. Suddenly a shot sounded at the entrance of the town and groups armed to the teeth appeared from all sides, surrounding the police station simultaneously with precision and speed.

The Navy radio was put out of action and before the poor private first class knew what was happening, he was tied to his chair. Lieutenant Martinez, surrounded by four men who were aiming their revolvers at him, begged them not to do him any harm; he would do whatever they asked. Someone wanted to kill him for being such a coward, but the orders of Patecuco were to avoid any unnecessary bloodshed. Out of pity for his family he was taken to the infirmary which had been turned into a prison for the police.

In the prisoners' exercise courts, they found only four sick men and a soundly sleeping private first class. As a joke, someone fired a shot from the policeman's own revolver near his head. But he cursed them because he wanted to keep on sleeping. He was shoved into the infirmary where they had already taken the others. The building was surrounded by tanks of gasoline and the most bloodthirsty prisoners stood guard at the door.

Once the most important tasks had been taken care of, the rebels entered the warehouse where they found weapons and boxes with new uniforms. Almost all of them dressed as policemen and began to act as such carrying two revolvers on their hips.

The colonists felt trapped and they didn't dare go out. Patecuco sent down a message that said: "Don't be afraid. We don't have anything against either the Franciscan Mission or the Colonists. We'll let the police take the heat. We're tired of their treatment of us. We want revenge and freedom".

The presence of such dangerous prisoners who were heavily armed did not calm anyone, so the townspeople gathered up the most indispensable belongings and took refuge in the mission church, hoping that the missionaries, a priest and a brother, would slow the daring of the worst ciminals.

The priest who was also the chaplain of the colony, had won a large following, so from the first he acted as a mediator. At the same time Patecuco showed great respect for the priest and for the people, which saved them all from a catastrophe. Patecuco, as we have said, was not a bloodthirsty man. He was never seen dressed as a policeman as were his companions, but rather wearing shorts, a shirt tied with a knot and barefoot. He carried his revolver hidden between his pants and his shirt, and with it maintained discipline among his 40 followers, who at times, were looking for revenge and ... sex.

The missionary recalled one of his first dialogues with the prisoners:

— "Why did you do this?"

—Because we don't want to continue living under the oppression of the "cops".

"What are your immediate intentions?"

— "To wait for the arrival of Cisneros's launch and another boat which is about to return from fishing and leave for the mainland, unless we can embark on a bigger boat on the way".

— "What are you going to do with the police?"

— For the moment, we have to be sure that we won't be attacked so that we can carry out our plans; then, we'll see".

— "And the colonists?"

— "Neither you nor they should be afraid; you can be calm".

It was a relief, but they could not be too sure. Finally, the priest and Patecuco came to an agreement:

— No prisoner could enter the church.

— No colonist would go out at night. During the day only the men would go out to their houses or their fields, but with permission from the priest.

This agreement gave them more peace of mind and maintained discipline. Patecuco made everyone comply with this agreement at all times. The situation of the police was more worrisome, because, without protection, they could be the object of a massacre. The missionary recalls the horrifying scene when he went to visit them.

"I entered the infirmary and froze at the sight in front of my eyes. There was the famous "Chico Panamá", a daring thief from Guayaquil entertaining himself playing a macabre game with the defenseless police: "Fall in line! Call off your numbers! One step back! Lie down! Stand up! All with shots into the air and at the floor very close to the feet of the unfortunate men. When I came in, the rebels stepped back and left them in peace.

I encouraged them the best I could but they asked for some protection. I offered to talk with the leader and did so. He agreed and ordered his men not to bother the police and they were left in peace".

At sundown, it seemed that the town was under a state of siege with sentinels on all the roads leading into it and a lot of prisoners wandering around the streets. Every one feared night fall. No one could rest in the darkness because of the prisoners' marauding, shouting, laughing and sporadic shots. They broke into some of the houses looking for clothing and liquor and then ended up in front of the church calling out indecent phrases. Some of them tried to go in but they always found the missionary ready to go between them:

"Stop! I am the only one in charge here and no one will come in unless it is over my dead body!"

That night only the children slept.

The second day of siege. February 11, 1958

On the second day the siege became more regular. The prisoners prepared food and checked the guns in groups. They threw the damaged ones into the sea. Others, feeling themselves in charge, showed off their arms and uniforms around town.

The bell that had been used to call the prisoners, now served to call the police. They had to fall in, as the prisoners did before, and perform "special services" for any reason amidst mockery and laughter. Finally they went into the improvised dining hall with "guards" in the front, the middle and behind, but with more discipline than the guards had had before. At the meals, the officers were served, but no one dared to eat, because they didn't know if the food contained poison or something similar. The rank and file police were served in the prisoners' plates with mocking courtesy. Fearful and humiliated, they returned without tasting the food, with lowered heads and some of them with tears in their eyes.

Meanwhile, the tension increased because the prisoners were getting bored with the lack of action and the long wait. On the other hand, Patecuco was on the verge of exhaustion since he hadn't slept in several nights. A calamity could be expected. A group of merciless men gathered secretly with "Perra Negra", the second in command, and pushed him to take over and assault the church. The missionary alerted Patecuco to the plan.

In the afternoon, while the leader was trying to rest, "Perra Negra" showed up with his followers and at gunpoint demanded that Patecuco give up the command. Patecuco jumped like a cat and, aiming his revolver, shouted: "I DON'T WANT TO!". "Perra Negra" stepped back, turned around terrified and disappared with his followers. Everyone gave a sigh of relief and Patecuco doubled the surveillance for the night that was drawing near.

Once again the people's anguish could be felt as they counted the hours and the sarcastic shouting in front of the church increased. The most perverse of the prisoners didn't leave the area, hoping to satisfy their base instincts.

The third day of siege. February 12

At dawn, they all looked out over the sea waiting for the fishing boats that should arrive. They first appeared as far off points. For the families of the fishermen, it was a moment of anguish, since they didn't know what would happen to them: At mid—morning the boats Teresita and Ecuador appeared with eight fishermen on board who were surprised when they didn't see anyone on the docks. Suddenly the pseudo—policemen appeared with shouts and shots:

"You are under arrest. We are free. Prepare to leave with us!" The preparations were slow since food had to be loaded and the hostages had to drive the boats. Near noon, everything was ready but nothing happenned. Were they planning to take revenge on the police?. Were they going to do something to the colonists?. Would Patecuco have enough authority to control so many criminals until the departure? Actually, they were waiting for a bigger boat that would allow them to risk crossing the ocean if necessary. The colonists feared a night of horror. An unexpected event precipitated the departure of the prisoners.

The electric plant was turned on at 5 o'clock every evening and kept on all for the colonists' protection. That afternoon when the man in charge entered, he noticed that something serious had happened. Some important pieces of the motors had been destroyed, apparently by a prisoner called "Maquinista" (mechanic). It was a warning that something was being planned. He came to warn the missionary and together they approached Patecuco, who realized the seriousness of the problem. Followed by a body guard, he faced Maquinista, a tall, thin, athletic young man and reprimanded him for his conduct. The young man, furious, took out his revolver and cocked it, as did Patecuco. A shot sounded and then another and another. Suddenly Patecuco doubled over, grabbing his stomach. The young man, thinking that he had wounded him, raced away, but Patecuco grabbed his bodyguard's revolver and began to chase him. His strategy when he had run out of bullets had been effective. Jnfortunately, Maquinista who hadn't been able to hit his target even once, half turned around and fired his last bullet which hit his persuer in the calf.. Everyone set off after the Maquinista, but he was a very agile and was able to hide in the brush. The injured man was taken to the church where the Franciscan brother like a professional nurse, took very solicitous care of him. The bullet hadn't touched any important bone or tendon. Patecuco stayed where he was for a while, but gave orders to embark immediately.

Before they set sail, they sacked Mr. Cisneros' store to get provisions. Patecuco was very alert and ordered that the police be kept under careful surveillance with Perra Negra himself in charge.

At 6 p.m. the 21 prisoners who had decided to leave began boarding with the four hostages who would sail the boat. The hostages' families were desperate because they were afraid they would never see them again. As their last act, the police were ordered into formation and under Perra Negra's command, they marched toward the church. There they were turned over to the priest and when the last one disappeared into the church, he gave a goodbye shout, spun around on his heels and ran to the boats.

When darkness fell and the silhouettes were lost out at sea, everyone returned to the church, since the rebellion was not yet over . The prisoners who remained on the island made their presence felt marauding around the area and shooting. Thus ended the 12th of February.

The Odyssey

The two boats headed west going around the southern end of the island to look for the fishing boat Viking, in which they could risk crossing the thousand kilometers that separated them from the mainland. Near midnight they came upon the fishing boats "Danubio" and "Bismark" who told them that the "Viking" was anchored in front of Punta Moreno (Southwest of Albemarle). At 4 in the morning they began the maneuvers to take over the Viking, but a shot was fired which alerted the owner, Victor López and infuriated Patecuco. He reprimanded the prisoner who had endangered the operation and explained to Lopez that he would have to accept the inevitable, but he assured him that his boat would be returned. The boat "Ecuador" and its two crewmen were freed while the "Viking" and the "Teresita" headed toward Tagus Cove where tourist yachts often set anchor. At midmorning they saw a medium–sized yacht which was anchored and disembarking passengers on the island. They prepared to board it. The two boats were steering parallel courses and they all had their weapons ready. They were a short distance away when several of them gave out a cry of alarm when they read on the bow: "California Military Academy". That word "military" and the great number of men on board, around 200 would have meant suicide, if they had attacked them. The rebels hid their weapons and sailed by, exchanging greetings.

They decided to spend the night drifting in front of Black Cove, but the next morning they awoke to their surprise that the currents had carried them out to open sea very near Roca Redonda northwest of Albemarle. They went on to James Island and the sites visited by American tourist yachts. They turned south and in front of Cape Napean, they made out the silhouette of a relatively small ship. Was it a fishing vessel or a Navy patrol boat? They didn't want to take any risks after the near disaster at Tagus Cove. So they approached until they could clearly distinguish:

"Valinda, CALIFORNIA", the elegant yacht of William Rodes Harvey.

In the darkness of the night, they took over the yacht which was only occupied by six people: Mr. Harvey and his wife, a friend who had boarded two days before, the chief machinist, a sailor who fortunately spoke Spanish and the cook. Once again, Patecuco's authority avoided calamity, while the captain of the Valinda skillfully managed the situation.

Before they left, they faced the dilemma of what to do with the boats: to sink them or allow them to leave with the danger that they would be given away. Since the promises that had been made did not seem to have any effect, Enrique Fuentes, the owner of one of the boats decided to go all or nothing.

"As for me— he said, sitting down in his boat— I will die here

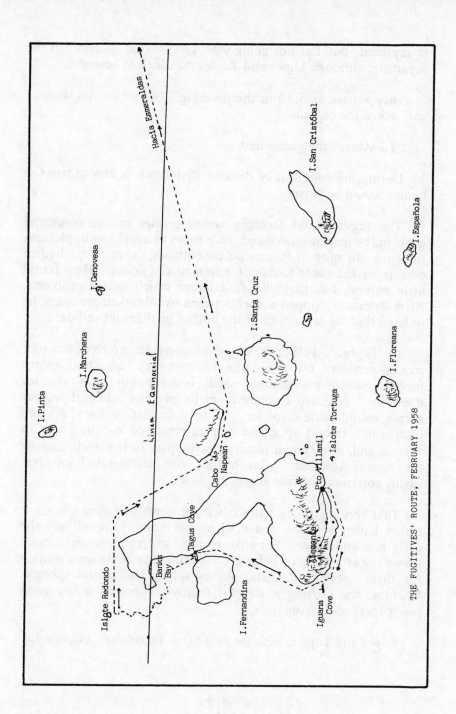

THE FUGITIVES' ROUTE, FEBRUARY 1958

Hacia Esmeraldas

I.San Cristóbal

I.Española

I.Genovesa

I.Santa Cruz

I.Marchena

I.Floreana

I.Pinta

Línea Equinoccial

Islote Tortuga

Pto.Villamil

Cabo
Napean

Islote Redondo

Tagus Cove

Banks
Bay

I.Fernandina

Iguana
Cove

in my boat, but I'm not going with you". That determined the departure, although Lopez and Tupiza remained as hostages.

They set sail at 5:30 in the morning. "Where do you want to go?" asked the captain.

"To Manta" they answered.

During the voyage they decided that Tumaco, in southern Colombia would be better.

The fugitives put strongly armed guards on the command deck, in the machine room and radio room to avoid any unpleasant surprises. In spite of Patecuco's precautions, the men searched all corners of the yacht looking for money and liquor. They found little money, but they did find liquor which caused problems. After Patecuco stopped a duel between two drunken prisoners, he ordered that the remainder of the bottles be thrown overboard.

On February 17th, they entered Esmeraldas, north of Ecuador around sundown, but a few minutes later they had a bothersome problem when innumerable small boats began to ask obvious questions. Patecuco forbade them to give any information, but silence would cause suspicion. So they decided to disembark and disappear. Only Lopez and Tupiza remained on the yacht to witness and, in a certain manner, participate in the celebration of the North Americans who hugged one another with joy after having gotten out of that adventure alive.

That very night the Valinda set out north to Panama, but not before having sent the first news by radio about the odyssey the party had undergone. For that reason, when they reached Panama on the afternoon of February 20, numerous boats were waiting for them with journalists, photographers and curious people. Ecuador, the Galapagos and the fugitives appeared in the great newspapers of the Americas.

Lopez and Tupiza, with the help of the Ecuadorian ambassador, were able to return to Guayaquil and from there to the Galapagos safe and sound. The fugitives spread out around Esmeraldas province, but were captured one by one during the following weeks and sent to the prison in Quito. During the implacable search and chase by the police, one of them was killed.

Meanwhile, in the Galapagos, the directors and the police were barely able to recover from the humiliation and they were relieved from their posts. They had to explain what had happened and above all the causes that led to the uprising. In their declarations, the Director and some of the guiltiest police tried to remove the blame from themselves, accusing the chaplain and some of the townspeople of having provoked the prisoners. It would be explained as a form of defense, but it hardly held a moral value. Although it is hard to believe, the famous lieutenant rose to a very high military rank.

Meanwhile, the town began a campaign to have the Penal Colony removed from Albemarle Island and out of the Galapagos. President Camilo Ponce decreed its supression in 1959. Thus ended a dark era in the history of the Archipelago, an era in which it was believed that islands were a comfortable and secure prison for the least desirable elements of society.

CHAPTER XI

GALAPAGOS : END OF A UTOPIA.

The North American Colony on San Cristobal. 1960

From time to time idealists who want to reorganize society according to their own ideas appear in this world.

These attempts are usually called utopias or simply crazy ideas; unfortunately, the end is always the same: frustration and failure.

The idea of an exemplary colony on the Galapagos Islands was forged in the mind of an asiduous science fiction reader after he read an article about life in the Galapagos. Fantasy and dreams did the rest. Why not organize a community on an island in the Pacific, guided only by the philosophy of science and scientific investigation? asked the promoter.

For a happy world, religious, political and moral motivations were unnecessary. This new project in the Galapagos would serve to show the world that such motivations were mainly problems. In his enthusiasm, he forged his plan which would have a name:

"FILIATE SCIENCE ANTRORSE"

and a simple and atractive slogan:

"TOGETHER WITH SCIENCE WE MOVE FORWARD"

a destination:

GALAPAGOS !

A marvelous site, isolated, almost unpopulated, but with all the conditions necessary for a colony dedicated to work, scientific investigation and community life.

And a base   for the project:

> " The scientific philosophy would guide them to a different kind of community life, to a scientific investigation at the world's service. It would also help them to understand animal structure and through it, human structure.
> The research and the laboratories would atract constantly greater economic support from advertisers and the scientific community. This would benefit the colonists, who, would be able to maintain the American standard of life on a far away island in the Pacific."

The psychological and social difficulties of such a different experiment could be overcome with the counseling of specialists from the universities. But, given the conditions of the island, the organization of the project and above all the selection of the personnel according to the principles of the phylosophy of science, its success was assured.

Who was the promotor of this fantastic plan?.

He was a definitive 35 year-old eccentric from Seattle , - Washington; an avid reader of science fiction who was very interested in the philosophy of science, although he had very little academic preparation. He had never finished high school; instead he had enlisted in the army with the hope of traveling to Alaska. When he became disillusioned with the north, he looked for a way out and managed to get discharged from the army for misconduct.

He claimed to be an atheist and an enemy of religious traditions. He was a racist and cynical about politics and governments. He believed that the colony in the Galapagos should be officially atheist and that there would be free love and democratic equality, although the males would have slightly more power. His confused ideas were reinforced when he found a university professor who backed his projects and offered to help with the preparation and planning.

The above named company is being formed under Ecuadorian law, and will be permanently located in the Galápagos Islands. It seems only right that a colony of scientific philosophists be located where Carles Darwin arrived at his theory of evolution. There is no need for anyone to give up their American heritage to participate in this venture.

COVER from the promotional bulletin of the utopian Galápagos Colony of 1959

The immediate tasks were:

— The elaboration and circulation of a pamphlet which, in a confusing fashion, presented the project: "Filiate Science Antrorse". Address/ 10640 Aqua Way, Seattle 88, Washington.

— Selection of the future colonists. More than 300 people responded with applications. The interviews were done almost exclusively by the promoter and the final decision was his. By his criteria, many of the applicants were not acceptable according to the previously established conditions, but he felt that the influence of his personality would finally change them.

— The capital required for investment in the project or the condition for the application was 2,500 dollars. In fact, payment of the money was the real condition for being admitted.

— The selection of the ideal site: Albemarle Island. They negotiated the purchase of 20,000 hectares in the area near Cartago Bay, south of Perry Isthmus. They considered it to be the ideal area for all kinds of crops. At the same time they could take advantage of the abundant wild cattle on the island, which, according to estimates, surpassed 70,000 head. They were an unending source of wealth. Besides, according to the reports, the sea was full of fish and on the beaches, the lobsters were within a hand's reach.

Someone must have given them some a d v i c e in time because although the high plains of Albemarle appear green at certain times of the year, there is no water there. They chose Chatham for obvious reasons.

— They planned to buy a boat for transportation, refrigeration equipment, and a fish processing plant along with small fishing boats.

— They would form teams for mass production of coffee and cacao, which would begin producing in four years with several harvests a year (!!!). They would also cultivate pineapples and other fruits.

— The installation of scientific laboratories of the the study of biology.

—The sources of wealth, according to the promoters, were numerous and with decisiveness and hard work they would be able to maintain the North American standard of living and obtain a better income.

Curiously, one paragraph added: "We will also obtain income from the sales of biological specimens to zoos all over the world. There are specimens available in the Galapagos that exist nowhere else in the world. Our business in this field is very good and we are already making the necessary contacts".

— "Some infrastructure would be necessary, such as wells for water, roads and buildings. Raw materials had to be acquired, such as wood. The latter would be easy to obtain from the supplies left at the American base on Baltra Island 15 years earlier in 1945 ". (!!!)

The planners did not take into account the Ecuadorian population already settled on the island or the real situation of the Archipelago, located 1000 kilometers from the coast with little communication with the continent at that time. Apparently all of their commercial plans looked only at markets in the United States and didn't take into account their rights and obligations with Ecuador.

There were 106 people (22 families and 14 single people) selected for the project. They had extremely diverse origins, education and character; there were workers from airplane factories, farmers, drivers, firemen, merchants, a janitor, a plumber and several teachers.

One of the few things they had in common was a general dissatisfaction with their lives and a desire to change and find a different horizon. The dream of colonizing a Pacific Island mixed adventure with a supposed economic opportunity, although none of them knew what they would encounter or their possibilities of success. In any event, these apprentice Quijotes handed over their quota and headed blindly along the road of utopía.

By the end of 1959 they had arranged the essential paperwork for migration with the Ecuadorian authorities. They were also preparing to buy an old tuna boat, which they would christen "Alert", for $ 3,500,oo.

The first group was ready to board, headed by the leader and promoter of it all, but the problems began at that moment. The "Alert" was not in satisfactory condition for sailing and the port authorities (U.S. Coast Guard) required them to make certain minimum repairs.

At last, on January 8, 1960, the "Alert" set sail from Puget Sound (Washington State) for the Galapagos. During the trip the ship had to take refuge in Californian ports several times because of bad weather and engine problems. Navigating from California to the Galapagos was a true martyrdom, but they arrived at Wreck Bay on Chatham on March 16,1960.

When the expedition landed on the island they all thought it would be very easy to settle and begin the life they dreamed of, as if they had just discovered an uninhabited planet. No one had told them that there were already people living there. Even though the population was small, it had been there for a long time. This improvisation and lack of knowledge turned the adventure into disaster.

On one side of the bay they found a refrigeration plant that had never functioned, but their leader planned to buy and repair it. About eight kilometers from the Port there was a plantation with approximately 64,000 hectares which they planned to buy to grow coffee.

The first concern of the colony was to abtain about 20 tons of lobster, immediately for the return voyage of the "Alert."

According to the lowest estimates, this would give them a profit of approximately $40,000. Unfortunately, none of newly arrived colonists knew where to find the lobsters nor how to capture them. Their abundance had been exaggerated and the local fishermen had neither the equipment nor the time to satisfy the demand. After they had caught a small quantity, the ship's refrigeration system broke down and could not be repaired.

Meanwhile the head of the colony had paid $30,000 for the refrigeration plant. However, when the people who were experts in that area arrived to examine it, they realized that it had deteriorated too much and was impossible to repair with their limited means.

The acquisition of land became more difficult because the Archipelago had been declared a National Park a short time before and regulations for property rights had not yet been drawn up. The conditions for sales depended on new laws yet to be passed by the Ecuadorian Congress.

The few attempts at cultivation failed for the most incredible reasons. Some crops were destroyed by the feral animals that wandered around the higher parts of the island. When they protected the fields with fences, exceptionally strong winter rains fell and washed away the seed and the plants.

Meanwhile in the mainland the news of the arrival of a "Yankee Invasion" produced a strong reaction which leftist movements used to their advantage. It was the period of effervescence after Castro's triumph in Cuba. (1)

(1) Leftist agitation was generalized in Latin America and intensely fought against by the CIA. The atmosphere that existed appears in the book "Inside the Company , Diary of the Cia" by ex-agent Philip Agee, 1960.

Groups of communist students threw rocks at the United States embassy in Quito and some leaders compared the "invasion of the Galapagos" with the "invasion of Texas" in the middle of the 19th. century.

The Second group of colonists were preparing to set sail in the "WESTERN TRADER", an old refrigerated ship which had been purchased for $32,500. More than 70 people with their possessions and working tools were trying to accomodate themselves in the uncomfortable ship for the long trip to the Galapagos. Again the California authorities detained the overloaded ship which was not in any condition to sail. Twenty eight people had to look for other means to travel to their destination.

When it seemed that everything was in order, this second group received the news that the Ecuadorian goverment had denied permission to import the machinery tax free. Since the cost of repairs and imprudent purchases had used up all of the group's reserves, the valuable cargo of tractors, small fishing boats, tools and a jeep had to be left in the port.

The voyage of this second group could not have been more miserable: there was a shortage of food, chaos reigned in the ship and no one directed anything. Many of the new colonists were near exasperation and even madness after five months of traveling, waiting and traveling again. Even those who had not reached the verge of madness were horrified by the mutual repulsion and lack of confidence that reigned in the group. Courtesy and even ordinary acts of politeness and consideration had disappeared. Agressiveness and bad humor replaced good manners. Little things such as cigarettes, disappeared as soon as their owner let them out of sight.

The prospects for a happy landing in Galapagos once more banished.

Even before they arrived in the Galapagos they received a petition from the first group to depose the original promoter for being incapable and impossible to deal with. They accused him of causing the disorder and improvisation, but especially of being arrogant and violent. He demanded the best for himself, but he acted like an overseer with the others. Ninety per cent voted for his deposition. In spite of this, shortly afterwards, the disqualified leader announced in the United States, a new project to colonize the Amazon. (!!!)

When the second group arrived on the island and heard the experience of the first group, disillusionment was widespread. There was no hope of buying land; the colony could not seem to find the right direction; the attitude of the local population towards them was negative because they were considered intruders. On the other hand, the possibilities of true colonization and lucrative commerce seemed very remote, given the distance of the markets, the lack of qualified laborers and the unavailability of machinery and spare parts. To top it all, the colonists began to fall ill, especially with dysentery and hepatitis.

The colonists were economically bankrupt and profoundly bitter. They could only try to think of ways to leave their exile as quickly as possible. They repaired the boats as best they could and set sail for the north. The "Alert" sank in Panamá, although all the passengers were saved. The "Western Trader" sailed on to México and was abandoned there, but one of the colonists and his family were able to repair it and continue on to San Diego, where it was sold for one third of its original price.

By January, 1961, all but one of the colonists had abandoned the island. They returned to their homeland after having spent their savings to begin from scratch. They felt a profound bitterness in their souls and a resentment against each other; against the one who had led them on this crazy project; against their companions in the adventure, in whom they had not found the openess nor the comprehension they had hoped for; against the Ecuadorian population who had taken them for simple invaders; and against themselves for having been so naive as to allow themselves to be taken in.

Utopias are expensive, not only in money, but above all in

energy and frustration. It took almost all of the participants a long time to recover from the traumatic experience of the colonizing adventure. All of them, but especially the second group, were left with the feeling that they had fallen to the level of HOMO HOMINI LUPUS (man is a wolf to men).

When one of the group was asked what he would least like in life, he answered "seeing one of my companions again". !!!!

PUERTO CHICO, Today PUERTO BAQUERIZO MORENO at Wreck Bay, San Cristobal Island.

CHAPTER XII

The Disappearance of "El Pequeño Pirata"

As the islands in the northern part of the archipelago have no water whatsoever, they have had few visitors in the past except for the fishermen from the islands and the tuna boats from California.

Schools of migrating tuna enter the islands' waters and right behind them follow the huge tuna boats, many times illegally.

The Galapagos fishermen catch codfish, especially from November to January, which is then sent to the mainland for consumption during lent and to be used in the preparation of "fanesca", a traditional lenten dish one of whose ingredients is dried cod.(1) They normally leave prepared to be out a long period of time because they alternate between fishing and drying the codfish out on the lava flows of certain islands.

Towards the end of 1967, a small fishing boat, "El Pequeño Pirata" left as usual for a long stay on the northern islands. It had a newly renovated engine, and food and water for four to six weeks, and a crew of five people, all family and friends who had worked together and knew the art of fishing and drying codfish.

The fishermen in the Archipelago all know each other and are always willing to deliver mail, and so each boat returns with news and messages for families left behind.

The Pirata's crew was excellent. They were all hard workers and they worked well together, a necessity on these long voyages. They had said good - bye to their families with the customary smiles and hugs and headed off towards the northern islands, Pinta, Marchena and Genovesa.

---

(1) Dried cod from Ecuadorian waters, also called "cabrilla" belongs to a distinct species of the North Atlantic oceans, and for that reason experienced a name change.

At the end of the first week, the families received news that all was well, by the end of the second the same but after that silence.

Two weeks later the relatives began to worry and questioned other fishermen that had been in the area but no one had any concrete news. One of them remembered having seen a fishing boat that was slowly heading towards the north but he couldn't say for sure if it was El Pequeño Pirata. They could not wait any longer for news and sounded the alarm. Fishermen criss-crossed the area without finding a trace. A patrol boat of the National Navy widened the search towards the north and the west but without results.

The only explanation was that it had sunk without leaving a trace. The families resigned themselves to the tragic reality that they would never see their loved ones again when the news arrived that El Pequeño Pirata was sighted in front of the Isla de los Cocos, near the coast of Costa Rica. The little fishing boat had been dragged by the currents of the northern archipelago. And there was something very strange on board; there were no signs of life. The captain that discovered El Pequeño Pirata sent a row boat over to inspect it and what they found shocked them even more. There was nobody on board and no signs of violence or problems. The boat's engine was still working perfectly, the hold had enough food and water for a couple of weeks, and the fuel tanks still had enough for a long voyage. How does one explain the disappearance of the whole crew? The closeness of Isla de Los Cocos leads one to believe that they might have decided to disembark there.

When the news arrived in Guayaquil, the Navy "Marines" were asked to solve the mystery. It was a very dynamic group and they took to the task enthusiastically. They left by transport ship right away and landed on the island determined to leave no corner of the it unexplored and if possible to clear up the mystery of El Pequeño Pirata. They worked all day and spent each night in an improvised camp in order to continue their search the following morning. They traversed thickets, dark ravines surrounded by hills and rocks, looking for a footprint or object that would help solve the mystery. They shouted hoping for an answer but only a distant echo was heard.

At the end of each day, the frustrated searchers report was the usual, nothing, absolutely nothing. They were certain that no one had even been on the island for many months. The closest coast-line was more than one hundred kilometers away, so the chances of them fleeing there were highly illogical as well as unlikely. They returned to Guayaquil with the sad conclusion that they would never know what happened to the men of "The Little Pirate."

Just when everyone had forgotten about this sad affair, some unexpected news arrived in Guayaquil. A Japanese vessel in route to Panamá had seen a light at night on Isla de Los Cocos and at dawn they saw no boat nearby.

The word spread and there were those that criticized the officers and sailors of the Navy, who in looking back all asked the same question, had they over looked some corner of the island? They were sure that they had searched everywhere but the only way to stop the rumors was to return to Isla de los Cocos.

A new search party was organized to clear up any doubts, de-termined to search every square foot of the island. What expla-nation would they find for the light on the island? Could it have been a boat passing by or a shipwreck?

They spread out all over the island in a systematic fashion, descending with ropes down cliffs and onto beaches in search of footprints. They examined the low tide areas but absolutely no-thing was found that would clear up the mystery. The image of that desolate island, its thickets, beaches and cliffs, and of "El Pe-queño Pirata" floating without direction was to remain forever etched in the memories of all those who participated in the search.

They left for Guayaquil.

It may never be known why and how they disappeared with-out leaving a trace but certainly the mysterious circumstances surrounding their disappearance encouraged all kinds of absurd explanations from collective insanity to sea monsters to even a new Bermuda Triangle.

The waters of the Galapagos have taken new victims, this time in the most inexplicable circumstances.

CHAPTER XIII

ALBEMARLE: THE ECUADORIAN MARINES PAY THEIR TRIBUTE

Survival exercises are frequent in the Armed Forces, especially for those troops chosen to carry out difficult tasks during wartime. The Naval Infantry or Ecuadorian Marines are a select body which was recently formed during the decade of the 60's. It was inspired by the North American and the English Commandos, but its vigor is born from the youthful spirit trying to form its own tradition. It has come to be highly appreciated and among its founders are men of the highest quality. Part of that tradition has been maintaining stict training, being good companions and knowing how to compete with the best men in making services, without ever losing their sense of humor or fresh view of life.

A typical exercise took place a few years ago. Together with other groups from the Army, the Marines were participating in commando exercises with instructors who had recently arrived from Vietnam, in the Toachi jungle on the western slopes of the Andes. The Marines impressed the "gringos" with their strong spirit, but also with typical youthful informality. In the midst of the exhausting exercises, which closely imitated a true campaign, they figured out a way to set up a tiny bungalow in the middle of the jungle. It became the center of happy gatherings in which even the instructors participated. Their surprise was even greater when the air was filled with rhythmic music in the early evening. Someone had added a small record player to his already heavy pack!

One of the survival exercises of the Ecuadorian Marines consisted of marches across entire provinces without provisions, where they had to cross the lines of supposed enemies who were determined to capture them at any cost. Other times they jumped with a parachute and had to arrive at a determined site by a certain time on their own. They are, in a few words, men who have been hardened by their efforts and in many years they have not had to admit serious failures.

Near the end of 1979, a combined exercise was organized in Galapagos with an amphibious landing, a march across the islands and possibly also some aid to the National Park in erradicating the feral goats which are a plague there. The march on Albemarle Island was estimated to be 28 kilometers through an unexplored zone. They thought that 36 hours would be sufficient for men going in formation, armed and carrying equipment. The estimate was logical if one considers that 28 kilometers can be covered in less than eight hours on a normal road. The batallion participating in this exercise was composed of 200 men. They did not all have the same experience, but they were in top physical condition and had high morale. The party included several sergeants, privates first class and marines. They were under the orders of four lieutenants and a doctor.

There were some deficiencies in the planning that were criticized later, but within a survival exercise these could be considered as a calculated risk. Unfortunately, the exercise was going to take place in an area of the National Park where it was not allowed.

They left Guayaquil in the middle of November, 1979, in a Navy ship and after three days of sailing, arrived in the landing area. On the way, the sea was rough and some of the men became seasick; this factor influenced later events.

The landing took place in mid—afternoon on Saturday, the 21st. The sea remained rough and under those circumstances it was too difficult to achieve a formal amphibian landing in an area with no beaches. Two squadrons of eighty men each arrived on the rocky coast with great difficulty. The third squadron remained on board because night had fallen and under the circumstances it would be suicidal to continue the landing. This was the other factor that was to influence later events.

The groups were organized on land and given instructions and passwords and the order to march, the squadrons began the march in semi-darkness in order to get away from the sea and find a place to spend the night. The temperature was pleasant, although later it became cold. There was no chance of rain so it was not necessary to set up a formal camp. The groups settled down to spend the night in an orderly fashion with their traditional discipline and seriousness.

It was a calm night: they did not hear a noise of the city nor the ship's engines, which had been so bothersome during the former nights, but only the waves of the sea breaking on the nearby coast. It was actually an overpowering silence for those who could not sleep for some reason. Minds flew to fantasy amidst such a mysterious realm of nature as that of the Galapagos, surrounded by volcanoes and monotonous gray vegetation. In reality they were in an area of recently formed active volcanoes, but they did not expect to witness an eruption that night.

At the specified hours they heard the passwords, the changes of the guard and then . . . silence!

At dawn, very early and after a campaing breakfast, they began the march, with the squadrons spaced about 500 meters apart. When the sun rose, nature took on a gray aspect that turned menacing as the hours passed. The bushes and rough brush were mixed with prickly cactus a n d these forced the men to make constant detours around them. By mid morning the vegetation was more and more sparse and in its place recent lava formations began to appear. The march became still slower. The time came when there was only lava and they had to cross it. The temperature was more than 104ºF; the sun shone relentlessly from a leaden sky and the rays reflected on the ground, increasing the heat radiation.

Some of the men who had been seasick aboard the ship were already dehydrated and desperately needed to drink water. They were confident that the short distance of 28 kilometers would not require too much effort. The march across volcanic fields can only be described by those who have done it. The lava seems to reflect the sun, the surface is extremely broken and slippery and with every step there is the danger of destroying shoes and legs. The sharp edges of the crack act like knives that cut boots and cause painful injuries.

At the end of the first day, Sunday, they had advanced a few kilometers and all were worried especially the officers. They cal - culated the chances for the next day, although they held stead- fastly to the idea that the lava fields would end soo. The squad- rons maintained their marching rhythm and distance, but some individuals began to fall behind. The second night was harder. The men kept turning over in their minds what was happening and many of them could n o t sleep. More than one had drunk all of their water rations and they were worried and anxious about the day to come. They would have preferred to advance towards their goal at night, but the lava was too dangerous.

The squadrons began to move very early in the morning at a fast pace to beat the sun, but once again the lava slowed their march; they had to take care of their boots and legs. Dehydration was increasing and the first symptoms appeared. Some of the men were like sleepwalkers, with dry throats, red eyes, and minds ob- sessed with the thought of water.

Towards midday the first fainting occurred, followed by loss of conciousness and even convulsions. . . The spirit of comraderie went to work at once to help those w h o had fallen , although some felt that they would soon be in the same condition. The doc- tor, loyal to his oath, attended all of them, but there was little he could do under the circumstances. The others, in ominous silence, tried to find strength in their convictions, looked for the vague shadow of the cactus, and hoped that things would get better.

By the afternoon, dozens of men were in poor conditions, al- though they kept their order and continued to advance. Forty hours had passed and they hadn't covered even half of the trial. The lava fields were interminable and there was no hope of finding even a drop of water. The weight of the equipment, the armament and the general bad feeling caused them to be irritable. Some of them discovered that they could wet their throats with cactus - - juice. It tasted like lye, but it was a relief.

The strengths or weaknesses of the men showed in those moments. Social life allows us to pretend to be something we are not, to play a role or show a facade; but when we are reduced to basic necessities, we appear as we really are, with our weaknesses or inner strengths. If we live with high values, we can resist many trials, but weak personalities break relentlessly. Thus, while many helped the weaker ones, others cursed, cried or isolated themselves in a nerve-racking silence .

The officers looked for solutions, but they always came back to the same point: the only solution was to continue towards the goal where the ship was waiting for them. Inside themselves, each one tried to solve that terrible unknown. If things continued as they were at the moment, they could fear the worst. Almost no one had his boots in good condition because of the effect of the knife-like lava but the worst affliction continued to be the lack of water.

A person can spend several days without eating, but very few without drinking. There are cases in history in which water has decided the luck of entire expeditions. Such was the case of the Athenians' retreat from the blockade of Syracuse which ended in a massacre when they threw themselves into the water; or the battle of Lake Tiberiades during the Crusades, when the astute Saladin, waited for the Western knights at the lakeshore, knowing they were desperate with thirst. The Arab lines broke, but the Crusaders went first into the lake. The last columns drank the water mixed with blood of their dead companions.

On this occasion, the group of officers decided to send four men with the most senior officer to look for help. The two squadrons remained behind with an officer in charge of each. They would continue to advance as the terrain permitted. Meanwhile the group looking for help left. The vanguard accelerated the pace, without worrying much about those who were falling behind. After all, they thought, the weak ones would be picked up

by the rearguard. The latter was under the command of an extremely valuable officer who maintained discipline and above all,
the morale of his men. The norms to be followed were clear: no one
should be separated from the group and they would all march at
the pace of the weakest. They would all help each other. This
attitude saved them from a tragedy of greater magnitude.

The third day was horrifying: almost no one had a drop of
water and thirst affected them all and drove several of them crazy.

A few fell into a coma after going into convulsions. Their boots
had disappeared and there was no solution other than wrapping
their feet in shirts and jackets, although in this way their bodies
were exposed to the thorns and brush.

The rearguard stayed together and picked up all of those from
the vanguard who were sick or had fallen behind. Those who were
weak leaned on others and those who had fallen into a coma were
carried on the shoulders of their companions. In a prudent decision, the officer ordered them to leave their weapons piled in a
visible place to be picked up later. Relieved of the weight, they
were able to help the weaker ones and they did.

While this drama was occuring on the lava fields of Albemarle,
the ship's crew was becoming alarmed. It was time for everyone
to be aboard and no one had appeared. That night the ship kept
its spotlights turned on to orient the lost soldiers and it sounded
its horn repeatedly. They tried to pick up some message by radio,
but in vain. They went over all the possible explanations and
suggested solutions.

At dawn of the fourth day, the ship's commander decided to
send help with the squadron which luckly had not taken part in
the march. They would take all of the water, rehydration salts,
and food that they could. When the march had been ordered and
they had been given precise instructions, they set out in the direction shown as quickly as the terrain allowed. Soon they realized
that it was not going to be easy: the undergrowth, the thorns, the
heat and the lava fields made them realize what their comrades
were suffering.

They walked all day without finding anyone; they inspected the area, checked the horizon, and shouted without receiving any response. . . Night came, and they continued to advance, conscious that they were going to save some lives.

The group in the vanguard heard the voices around nine at night. The encounter was undescribable. They all flung themselves on the water containers with desperation, not thinking of anyone or anything. Only one of the rescue team was able to escape from that attack and take his canteen to the more numerous group of the rearguard. One canteen!

Officer Yepez of the rearguard ordered the men to fall in line and gave one sip to each man. One sip! Some did not get even that. In any case, this revived them since they believed that salvation was near. They slept in groups, more tranquilly, since they had the sensation that it would be the last night of that terrible ordeal.

At dawn, panic set in because several groups felt abandoned: the vanguard had left, not worrying about their men, nor those who had arrived the night before. Left to their luck, they reacted with their instincts of selfpreservation. They left by the shortest path, sure that their goal, the ship, was waiting for them nearby.

The rearguard continued picking up those who were left behind: they were exemplary for their bravery, organization, solidarity and companionship. They would arrive half-dead, but they would arrive together.

Eight men woke up in the morning and found themselves alone. Among them was a sailor who had arrived with the water the night before. Sure of the route, he offered to guide them. In a few hours, they would be at the ship, he assured them. They set out along the trail.

By midday they hadn't even seen the sea, which seemed strange. That night they slept together, unable to explain the situation: they should have at least been in sight of the ship by that time. At dawn they began the march optimistically, since they could not be far away. They climbed a hill and were able to see the ocean, but at a great distance. It would be impossible for them to arrive that day. They fell asleep very tired and devastated by hunger and thirst, since they had consumed all the food and water they had.

The following morning the eight men finally arrived at the ocean, but where was the ship? It was not anywhere in sight. They walked towards the north and then   toward the s o u t h without seeing anything, but with a growing uneasiness, especially the guide, who was totally confused. When they began doubting what they should do, they made out a boat sailing a short distance from the beach. They shouted, but nobody heard them. Since it was their only hope, they followed a parallel course, trying to get its attention. Some of them collapsed and stayed behind, but two of them continued the anguished race. The boat finally stopped and let down a small launch, but nobody had noticed the desperate soldiers. The last soldier in the group threw himself into the sea and swam in the direction of the boat. When his strength was almost exhausted and he was sinking into the sea, he gave a last shout which luckily was heard. They came to save him. It was a group of tourists who were approaching the Island. It was an illegal visit, but at that moment, a providential one that saved the men's lives. Soon they returned to go back to the ones who had collapsed and were lying at intervals over a long distance. Only one, Alvarado, did not appear anywhere.

After the men had satisfied their hunger and thirst, they asked where they were. The response left them cold: they were on the eastern side of the island. The guide had taken the wrong direction and they had retraced their tracks. Without the providential tourist boat, they would surely have perished. They reached the ship by sea !!

The other groups also arrived in the most diverse manners, except, of course, the rearguard, which came slowly, but to - gether. The last men arrived on the ninth day, totally exhausted.

Some of them had come from the north and others from the south. Some were even found by helicopters, since, by that time, the Chiefs of Staff had come with everything they had on hand to rescue the lost marines.

The group that had gone in search of help arrived on the fourth day, after a great effort in which more than one was victim of dehydration.

Everyone was on board, except Alvarado, and they could not explain his disappearance. With the help of a helicopter, they followed his trail, but to their surprise the first thing that appeared was his clothing, which had unexplainably come off. Had he discarded it? A couple of days later his body was found at the bottom of a cliff. He was dead. He was the only victim, but all knew that without a series of providential events, the tragedy would have been much greater.

The days passed: the men, however, will never forget that exercise, which was planned as one among many and which became a living hell. For the majority, it was an experience that showed certain revealing details of human nature: the heroic and the miserable; companionship in the highest degree and egoism in its worst form. It was an occasion to find themselves, with their most intimate values or their spiritual emptiness. It was a macabre trial, but if it did not entail so many risks for human life, it would be worthwhile to repeat it with the object of evaluating the men and getting to know them as they really are. It becomes so easy to live with simple facades and to fool oneself in the midst of a society that lives and judges by appearance.

In the inquiries that followed, those who deserved it were congratulated and those who had not done their duty were criticized. But beyond all criticism and commentary, a valuable experience, in which they found themselves, remained in their conscience.

IMPRESO EN "GRAFICAS ORTEGA"
TELEFONO: 545-150
QUITO - ECUADOR